Women of Prayer

GETTING TO KNOW GOD THROUGH THE PRAYERS OF BIBLE WOMEN

Praise for Women of Prayer

Sharon Wilharm has a heart for women—today's women and women of the Bible. In her new Bible study, *Women of Prayer*, Sharon guides learners in a beautiful blend of the two. By examining women of the Bible in-depth, she challenges us to dig deep into the Word of God, discover biblical insights from everyday women of Scripture, and to apply the truths of God to our life situations. Thanks for taking us on this journey, Sharon!
—**Brenda Harris**, woman of God, wife, mother and grammie, Prayer/Communications Associate, Kendrick Brothers Productions

The prayers of women have been shaping the world for years. Sharon Wilharm brings the power of prayer to life with her *Women of Prayer* Bible study. Whether you are looking to learn more about prayer or you have a study group you'd like to lead, the *Women of Prayer* Bible study will inspire you. As I read this study I was reminded of the contribution that women have made through prayer and I was encouraged to be a woman of prayer in a greater way.
—**Monica Schmelter**, host of *Bridges*, Christian Television Network

I have read and heard stories on women of the Bible for years but this book on women of prayer is very insightful. Sharon has truly written a life-changing prayer book. You can learn to trust God beyond your imagination. The podcasts and blog posts are a great addition to this book as well. I highly recommend this anointed book and encourage you to experience the blessed life that God wants you to have.
—**Lisa Hooks**, Power Fueled Living Ministries

Sharon's Bible study layout is a unique structure that helps the reader learn about the women who we often pass over as we read Scripture. Sharon changes that for us, allowing us to read and meditate on these women who are often overlooked. She focuses in on them and shows us how God interacts with every story. This study leads us through the lives of many women in a manner where we reflect upon our own lives and faith. Each reader will find at least one woman who she relates to through this study. The Lord will encourage, convict, and remind us of how much he loves women and will use us for his purposes! Thanks, Sharon, for this much-needed Bible study.

—**Tika Scoles**, Women's Ministry Director, Northside Baptist Church, Murfreesboro, Tennessee

Women of Prayer by Sharon Wilharm is a book about women in the Bible who knew God in a personal way. It's written to women about women and how God continues to speak to us through his Word. Studying *Women of Prayer* with the Scripture is teaching me how to go deeper and by staying with the same woman every day for a week, it's teaching me how to ask God questions that allows me to hear from him. I highly recommend *Women of Prayer* as an individual Bible study first, then as a group study. I love the way *Women of Prayer* is written in a way that I can personalize it to benefit my spiritual journey.

—**Sue Z. McGray**, Christian Author and Speaker, *Becoming Visible* and *Life-Changing Encounters and Divine Appointments* www.suezmcgray.com

Sharon Wilharm has a heart for women to know God more. In *Women of Prayer*, she takes us on a fascinating journey into the lives of women in Scripture to help us dig deeper and seek biblical truth applicable to our own lives. The format flows so well and you'll love the leader's guide included in the back! I highly recommend this study for women seeking fresh revelation, a richer prayer life, and to know God more.

—**Doris Swift**, author, speaker, and host of the award-winning *Fierce Calling* podcast

Sharon is a powerful communicator—gifted in diving deep into the recesses of hearts to bring solid solutions for everyday life situations to her readers and audiences. It's an honor to endorse this book because I know your life will never be the same—in the best of ways!

—**LaTan Murphy**, award-winning writer of *Courageous Women of the Bible (Overcoming Fear and Insecurity for A Life of Confidence and Freedom)*

Women of Prayer

GETTING TO KNOW GOD THROUGH THE PRAYERS OF BIBLE WOMEN

SHARON WILHARM

ELK LAKE PUBLISHING INC

PUBLISHING THE POSITIVE
Plymouth, Massachusetts

A Christian Company
ElkLakePublishingInc.com

Copyright Notice

Cover and Interior Design: Lana Ziegler, Derinda Babcock
Editor(s): Peggy Ellis, Deb Haggerty

PUBLISHED BY: Elk Lake Publishing, Inc., 35 Dogwood Drive, Plymouth, MA 02360, 2022

Library Cataloging Data

Names: Wilharm, Sharon (Sharon Wilharm)

Women of Prayer / [Sharon Wilharm]

266 p. 23cm × 15cm (9in × 6 in.)

ISBN-13: 978-1-64949-718-5 (paperback) | 978-1-64949-719-2 (trade hardcover) | 978-1-64949-720-8 (trade paperback) | 978-1-64949-721-5 (e-Book))

Key Words: Women of the Bible, Women's Bible study, Prayer, Bible women, Christian women, Old Testament women, New Testament women

Library of Congress Control Number: 2022945562Nonfiction

Dedication

To my mother, who gave me my first Bible women devotional that launched my fascination for women in the Bible

Table of Contents

Acknowledgments

This project would not be possible if not for the never-ending encouragement and support from my family. To my parents, thank you for your godly influence and instilling Christian values in us. To my husband, thank you for allowing me to follow God wherever he leads, and always providing unlimited support. To my daughter and son-in-law, thank you for being a sounding board, giving your thoughtful opinions whenever asked. I'm blessed to be surrounded by a family of cheerleaders.

To my Dig Deeper colaborers in the Lord, I'm forever grateful for your passion for Bible study and challenging me to dig deep in the Word.

To Springfield Baptist Church women who came to my luncheons and prayer retreats, thank you for joining me as we studied together and learned about Bible women and prayer.

To my Every-Other-Wednesday-Morning Bible study group, thank you, sweet ladies, for your friendship and encouragement and for your enthusiasm for studying women in the Bible.

To all my wonderful All God's Women listeners and followers, thank you for allowing me the privilege of sharing with you my passion for women in the Bible.

To Marnie Swedberg, thank you for all you do to support Christian women speakers, for connecting me to Jenne Acevedo and for introducing me to Elk Lake Publishing. And to Jenne, thank you for all your help in getting my book proposal ready to submit.

To my Elk Lake Publishing team of Deb Haggerty, Peggy Ellis, Judy Hagey, and Derinda Babcock, thank you for all you've done to help bring this Bible study vision to life.

To each woman who reads this book and participates in this study, I pray that God uses it to speak to your heart, to minister to your needs, and to impact your life in a mighty way. May you fall in love with Jesus and get to know him in a more personal way.

Introduction

Prayer should be the most natural thing we do, but it isn't. We make praying way more complicated than it needs to be, primarily because we don't understand God's character and how he works.

I know. I've been there.

Through the years, I've allowed into my head some mixed-up ideas about prayer, and for a time, I let them sabotage my prayer life. Unfortunately, I had no clue that anything was wrong because my misconceptions were based on advice Christian leaders had given me. It wasn't until I became serious about Bible study that I realized many of my views on prayer didn't agree with what I found in the Bible.

In high school, an amusing anecdote by a missionary reminding us to not forget to pray for people struck a chord with me. I began worrying something bad would happen to people if I didn't remember to pray for them. This concern put a lot of pressure on my prayer life as I tried to go through a checklist each time to include everyone I could think of.

In college, a leader told us to "be careful what you pray for." I took that to mean if I prayed the wrong words, God would send bad things because that's what I'd prayed for. The pressure increased as I strove to make sure I not only prayed for everyone but stressed over praying the perfect prayers for them.

For years, my favorite platitude was, "When God closes a door, look for a window." How many times have you heard that advice or even offered it yourself? What horrible advice it is, but we do see examples of it in Scripture. For instance, when Sarai got tired of knocking on a door that wouldn't open, she found a window to go through. What a mess that caused. When God closes a door, there is a reason he doesn't want us to go there. He certainly doesn't want us crawling through windows like a common thief.

The problem with prayer is we don't know God like we think we do. We may think we're his biggest fan, but we have a superficial understanding of him. We get secondhand information which gives a distorted picture of God's character. For effectual prayer, we need to truly know him on a personal level.

That's what I want for you—to get to know God as more than a superficial figurehead. I want you to get past a shallow relationship and get to know him on a deeper level so your days are one continuous prayer conversation. You can accomplish this by studying his Word and getting to know him intimately.

Most of the psalms were written by David, who the Bible refers to as a "man after God's own heart." We know he wasn't perfect and, in fact, failed quite miserably. David committed adultery and murdered a man. So, what distinguished him as a man after God's own heart?

David prayed constantly. He trusted God with whatever he was going through. He knew God intimately because he communicated with him through good times, bad times, and everything in between.

That is our goal, not to be perfect, though that's certainly a desirable goal, but rather to get to know God in the most intimate of ways so we're comfortable going to him wherever we are and whatever we're going through.

When that happens, you don't have to think about praying, for prayer comes naturally. You can't stop yourself because there's so much you want to talk to him about. Everywhere you turn is a reminder of him. You want to discuss everything with him. When no one else is there for you, you know you can run into his outstretched arms, and he will comfort you in a way no one else can.

For this study, I've chosen women in the Bible who knew God in a personal way. As we delve into their experiences, we'll discover how similar their stories are to our own.

Through this study, we will become acquainted with who God is and what he desires for us. We will look at women in the Bible who interacted with God or had conversations with Jesus. As we study those stories, we'll figure out how they apply to us. We will learn about God's character, his thoughts, his timing, his methods, and his heart. We will come away feeling more like a friend than just a fan.

What I love about Bible study is that the more I learn about God, the more I realize how amazing he is. As you spend your days reading Scripture and talking with God, may you find yourself falling in love with him. I pray your time in this study leads to a lifelong love affair with Yahweh, the One True God.

How to Use This Book

Welcome to *Women of Prayer*. Prayer is a personal activity, so I've designed this book in such a way that you can personalize your studies to suit your unique needs. This is not a fill-in-the-blank kind of Bible study where each question has a right or wrong answer. I'll show you how to study on your own and reach your own conclusions. I know that sounds a little scary, but I'll walk you through the process step-by-step until you discover for yourself how liberating Bible study can be on your own.

You don't have to worry about covering massive amounts of material. We go deep instead of going broad. You will read and reread passages until they come to life for you—and you discover new insights.

If you prefer having accountability and meeting together with other women, I've included a leader's guide with group activities and suggestions to guide your time together. However, I recommend you first go through the study alone, then invite other women to join you as you go through it a second time. You'll be amazed at how much more you'll discover when you read the exact same Scripture multiple times.

Here's our weekly schedule. Each week we zoom in on a specific Bible woman and her interaction with God.

Day 1: Her Story

You'll be introduced to the woman of the week and read about her interaction with God.

Day 2: Her Story in Context

You'll read Scripture passages before and after her interaction with God to put her story in proper context. In some cases, the study will take you to other chapters and even other books in the Bible which provide background information or show repercussions from her actions.

Day 3: Dig Deeper

You'll read the original passages but in a different Bible translation. This will help you notice details you may have missed in the first reading.

Day 4: Make it Personal

You'll learn to use resources to help you answer any questions you might have about the material you've studied. This is your opportunity to truly personalize your study and chase after any rabbit trails God might lead you on.

Day 5: Compare and Contrast

You'll take what you've learned and apply it to a different woman in the Bible with a similar interaction with God.

Each week you'll find these elements:

- An introduction to the week's Bible woman
- A Scripture memory passage with suggestions to help you memorize Scripture.
- Five days of personal study activities
- Daily review questions to guide your study.
- Prayer prompts
- Suggested resources for further study
- Guidance for group time

What you'll need:

- Bible
- Journal or notebook
- Pack of index cards

Optional:

While it's nice to have your own personal reference materials, each of these resources can be found at your local library or church library.

- Study Bible
- Parallel Bible (in print or online)
- Commentaries (in print or online)
- Bible dictionary
- Women of the Bible books
- Access to podcasts or blogs

Note: Throughout the study, I reference podcasts and blogs as optional activities. These can be accessed via a smartphone or home computer. I have podcast episodes and blog posts you can check out for each of the women we study. They're available at my website at www.sharonwilharm.com. You can either listen or read, whichever is your preference.

—Chapter One—
Hagar

Hagar's story used to make me feel uncomfortable. I felt sorry for her because she was such a victim of Sarai and Abram's drama, but as I studied her more deeply, I realized that, though Hagar was a victim, she was victorious and blessed by God.

Hagar was an Egyptian slave purchased by Abram to be Sarai's handmaiden. She didn't choose to be a slave. She had no choice.

Though Abram and Sarai were God-fearing individuals, they didn't always behave in a godly manner. In fact, they tended to get caught up in their own insecurities—with no regard for the impact their actions might have on others.

Hagar's life story hinges on the insecurities of Abram and Sarai. They journeyed to Egypt due to a famine in their land. Had they trusted in God to provide, they would have never entered Egypt nor acquired Hagar. Had they trusted God when he said he would send them a son, Sarai would have never given Hagar to Abram as a second wife, and he would have never agreed to it. Had Sarai not been riddled with jealousy when Hagar conceived and grew prideful, she wouldn't have taken Hagar's attitude personally, humbling Hagar until she fled for her life.

Sarai's problems created a bad situation for Hagar. Yet had she not run away from Sarai, she would have missed a face-to-face meeting with her Savior.

In the wilderness, God revealed himself to Hagar. Hagar was a pagan servant. In the world's eyes, she was little more than property. She was nobody.

Yet, she was somebody to God. He loved her and cared about her. He reached out to her, showed compassion for her, and encouraged her with a word of prophecy.

DAY ONE: HER STORY

God had promised Abram he would be a father of nations, but years passed. Despite God's promise, Abram's wife Sarai remained barren.

Sarai grew tired of waiting for God and took matters into her own hands. Deciding God needed her help to bring about his prophecy, she offered up her handmaiden Hagar as a second wife or concubine for Abram. Even though the practice of servant surrogates was an accepted custom and a legal option for barren wives, Sarai's interference didn't help anyone. Instead, she caused heartache for all involved.

Hagar must have been a trusted servant and well-liked by Sarai, or she wouldn't have chosen her to be Abram's second wife. But as soon as Abram slept with Hagar and she conceived, the status quo shifted.

Hagar knew about God's promise to Abram. Since Sarai was barren and Hagar pregnant, surely she was to be the one to bear the promised seed. Realizing this, Hagar grew prideful and looked at Sarai with contempt. She overstepped her position, acting as the superior to her mistress.

Genesis 16:6 tells us that Abram gave Sari permission to do to Hagar what she thought best, "Then Sarai dealt harshly with her, and she fled from her."

From our modern interpretation, we get the impression Sarai was abusive to Hagar, but if we look up the Hebrew word for "treated," we learn it means Sarai humbled her. In other words, Sarai made clear to Hagar, that though she was bearing Abram's child, she was still Sarai's servant, and as such was to treat her with respect. Not wanting to be humbled, Hagar ran away.

Hagar was on her way back to Egypt, her homeland, when the angel of the Lord found her by a spring of water near Shur.

Though he knew the answer, the angel asked Hagar where she was coming from and where she was going. He listened to her answers then told her to return to Sarai and submit to her.

But then He said,

> The angel of the LORD also said to her, "I will surely multiply your offspring so that they cannot be numbered for multitude." And the angel of the LORD said to her, "Behold, you are pregnant and shall bear a son. You shall call his name Ishmael, because the LORD has listened to your affliction. He shall be a wild donkey of a man, his hand against everyone and everyone's hand against him, and he shall dwell over against all his kinsmen." (Gen. 16:10–12)

To a free-spirited woman longing for freedom, God's words were exactly what she wanted to hear. Her son would be strong and independent, fighting his own battles, but remaining close to his family. God spoke Hagar's love language.

This pagan woman was alone in the wilderness, and God sought her out, offering her a prophecy of encouragement.

Though Scripture indicates Angel of the Lord, this was no mere angel. He addressed her personally when he said, "I will multiply your descendants," letting us know this was God himself seeking out this slave woman.

I love how Hagar responded, calling him *El Roi* which means, "The God Who Sees Me," and marveling she was able to see the one who saw her.

Hagar humbled herself and returned to Abram and Sarai, but fourteen years later, she was again in the wilderness, this time with her son Ishmael. Though she was convinced they were about to die, God revealed himself to her again.

Both Hagar and Ishmael were famished, languishing in the desert with no food or water to sustain them. They were weeping helplessly when God called down from heaven, telling Hagar not to fear but to lift Ishmael and hold him by the hand, for he would be a great nation. Then God opened her eyes to a nearby well with water to save them.

Though their situation looked hopeless, God had not forgotten Hagar and her son. God saw Hagar. He knew who she was. He saw what she was going through. And he cared for her. When all hope was gone, he came through for her.

Opening Prayer

Begin today's study by praying for God to help you understand Hagar's story.

Scripture Reading

Read Genesis 16:1–16; 21:9–19.

As you read, feel free to underline or highlight verses that jump out at you and/or make notes in your journal. If you make notes, be sure to date your notes and include Scripture references so you can come back at a later point and see what God was teaching you.

Review Questions

Each Bible study is unique. I've included review questions, not for you to feel obligated to write out answers, but rather to guide your study. They are designed to help you look for details you might otherwise miss. Ideally, as you read your Scripture, you'll write down your own questions that arise, and then as the week progresses, you can seek the answers to these and your own questions.

Where was Hagar from?

Why did Sarai offer Hagar as a second wife for Abram?

Why did Hagar leave Abram and Sarai the first time? Why did she leave them a second time?

Where did God find Hagar?

What did God ask Hagar?

What did God promise Hagar?

How did Hagar respond to God?

What did Hagar call God?

In your journal write down your own questions that come to mind as you read.

Scripture Memory Passage

O LORD, you have searched me and known me! You know when I sit down and when I rise up; you discern my thoughts from afar. (Ps. 139:1–2)

Read Psalm 139:1–2 aloud. How does it tie in with Hagar's story?

Closing Prayer

Write a prayer based on Psalm 139:1–2.

DAY TWO: STORY IN CONTEXT

God gave Abram a command and a promise. He told Abram to leave his country and go to a land that God would show him. Then he told Abram he would make him a great nation, "I will bless those who bless you, and him who dishonors you I will curse, and in you all the families of the earth shall be blessed" (Gen. 12:3).

Abram reached Canaan, and God made clear to him this was where he was supposed to be. Then famine hit. Rather than trusting God to provide for their needs, Abram went to Egypt. Leaning on his own wisdom rather than God's ability to provide for their safety, Abram concocted a lie to protect himself but put Sarai in an awkward position.

During Abram and Sarai's time in Egypt, Pharaoh blessed Abram with livestock and servants. This is likely when they acquired Hagar.

Abram and Sarai left Egypt and settled in Canaan, but the promised son still didn't come. Sarai remained barren. Eventually, Abram and Sarai second-guessed God. They figured God needed their help to make his promise come true. This is where Hagar came in.

Opening Prayer

Ask God to give you clarity and wisdom as you delve into Hagar's story.

Scripture Reading

Read Genesis 12:1–20; 15:1–21.

Additional Reading (for further study): Genesis 17:1–27; 18:1–15

Review Questions

What did God promise Abram in Genesis 12:2–3?

How old was Abram when he took Sarai and Lot and started to the promised land?

What did God promise Abram in Genesis 12:5?

Why did Pharaoh give livestock and servants to Abram?

What did God promise Abram in Genesis 15:4?

How might Hagar's life have been different had Abram and Sarai not gone to Egypt?

What idea of God might Hagar have had based on what she witnessed in the life of Abram and Sarai?

Scripture Memory Passage

Write Psalm 139:1–2 on an index card. Tape the card on your bathroom mirror or somewhere else where you'll see it throughout the day.

Closing Prayer

Pray that God will direct your paths and protect you from making unwise decisions.

DAY THREE: DIG DEEPER

We think of prayer being us going to God, but sometimes God comes to us, like God chasing after Jonah or greeting Mary. In this case, he sought out Hagar not just once, but twice.

When Hagar ran away from Abram and Sarai, she was certainly not looking for God. In fact, after being treated harshly by God's chosen couple, she likely had no interest whatsoever in their God. But though she fled, God personally sought her.

He opened the conversation with small talk, asking her where she was coming from and where she was going. Then he launched into his purpose in reaching out to her.

God told Hagar to return to Abram and Sarai. He knew how hard that would be, so he encouraged Hagar by telling her about her child and what he would become.

Hagar wasn't used to anyone going out of their way for her. Imagine her surprise and excitement that the God Who Sees saw her. She may have been insignificant and disposable to everyone else, but God valued her.

Hagar was doubly blessed when God came after her again, fourteen years later.

When Hagar first met God, she was running away. Though she had been angry and hurt, God gave Hagar hope for a better future. When she met God a second time, circumstances were more dire. Hagar was preparing to die. All hope was gone.

Just as God had seen Hagar stopping for water on her way back to Egypt, he heard her and Ishmael crying in despair. Like before, he opened with small talk, asking Hagar what ailed her. Then he told her not to be afraid. He told her to go hold her son. Then he gave her a promise for the future. He reminded her what he'd said before, that Ishmael would father a great nation.

God concluded their time together by opening Hagar's eyes to a nearby well of water.

Opening Prayer

Pray that God will open your heart to hear his voice.

Scripture Reading

Reread Genesis 16:7–13 and 21:16–19, this time using a different translation of the Bible. If you usually use a traditional version such as King James or English Standard Version, try reading in a modern translation like New Living Translation or Good News Translation. If you first read from a modern translation, read from a traditional version. Note any differences in the terminology.

The Bible is the living Word of God. You can read a passage over and over, and each time it's like reading each verse anew. You discover details you missed before, see familiar stories in a different light, and understand what previously didn't make sense. Scripture that seemed unrelated to your life will connect with you in unexpected ways. How exciting it is when that happens.

Perhaps you already have a variety of Bibles. If not, you may want to invest in a Parallel Bible which provides multiple versions side by side for comparison. Another option is using online resources. My personal favorite is Bible Hub. Other options are Bible Gateway and Blue Letter Bible. Each website allows you to read the same Scripture in multiple translations.

Review Questions

As we delve into Scripture more deeply, we often find ourselves asking "why" questions. We want to understand what motivated men and women of the Bible to act the way they did. What were their thoughts? Why did God respond in such a manner? How does all that we read relate to us?

We only know what the Bible tells us, but by pondering deeper questions, we receive a clearer picture of God and our relationship to him.

Why did God come after Hagar when she was running away from Sarai?

Why did he ask her questions when he knew the answers?

What command and promise did God give Hagar?

Why did God give Hagar a prophecy about her son?

Why did Hagar obey God?

Why did Hagar forget God's promise for Ishmael?

Why didn't Hagar call out to God?

Why does Scripture say God heard Ishmael's cries, but he called out to Hagar?

Why did God send Hagar back the first time, but not the second time?

Why did God only speak to Hagar when she was in the wilderness and not with Abram and Sarai?

Scripture Memory Passage

Every time you see your memory card, read the verse aloud.

Closing Prayer

Thank God for being El Roi, the God Who Sees. Thank him for seeing you wherever you are.

Day Four: Make it Personal

At first glance, we may not share much in common with Hagar. She was an Egyptian slave-turned-concubine whose son fathered a nation. Though our circumstances may be vastly different, she experienced many of the same situations and emotions we deal with today.

Hagar was ripped away from her native land and made to live the life of a nomad. Have you ever been forced to move against your will? Have you ever felt like a nomad, moving from city to city, house to house?

Hagar was at the mercy of others. She had little control over her own life. Have you ever felt as if your life was out of control? Do others make decisions that affect your well-being?

Hagar felt invisible as if no one saw her or cared about her. Have you ever felt that way?

Hagar was abused by those who were entrusted to care for her. Have you ever faced mistreatment from those you trusted?

Hagar ran away from her difficult situation. Have you ever run away from life? Have you ever wanted to run away?

Hagar reached the point where she gave up the fight. She lost hope. Have you ever given up, convinced that all hope was gone?

Opening Prayer

Pray for God to continue teaching you and showing you new insights as you study Hagar's story.

Scripture Study

Study Hagar's story using reference materials. There are many ways to accomplish this. Pick one that works for you. Or do several. Regardless of how you choose to study, be sure to search for answers to any questions you've written earlier in the week.

- If you have a study Bible, look up Genesis 16 and 21. Read each study note on the bottom or side of the pages. If they reference other passages, read those as well.
- If you have a Bible commentary, look up the passages to see what that commentator says. You can also find free Bible commentaries online.
- Use an online source (such as Bible Hub) to find sermons about Hagar. Read a sermon or two about her.
- Listen to my *All God's Women* podcast episodes or read my blog posts about Hagar.
- Search on your favorite podcast platform to find other podcast episodes about Hagar.
- Do a Pinterest search for blogs and other resources about Hagar.

You may find researching becomes addictive. You notice a reference in one source, which leads you on a rabbit trail to look up something related, which leads to another source. Research is exciting and personal. What jumps out to you may be completely different from what someone else notices. God does that. He knows what you're going through and will speak to you in a personal way through your reading and studying of the Bible.

As you read and study Hagar's story, make notes of anything you find interesting and want to remember.

Review Questions

The Bible isn't just an ancient book about a bunch of people who lived a long time ago. God continues to speak to us through his Word. Studying Scripture and asking questions allows us to hear from him.

What is the significance of Hagar's story in the Bible?

How are you like Hagar?

What can you learn from Hagar's story?

How did God show his love for Hagar?

What did Hagar learn about God's character?

How can you find comfort in God's treatment of Hagar?

Think of times in your life when you experienced "The God Who Sees."

How does it make you feel to know that God is always watching over you, aware of all that is going on in your life?

How can Hagar's story help you in your prayer life?

Scripture Memory Passage

Can you say Psalm 139:1–2 by memory yet? If not, keep working on it.

Closing Prayer

Thank God for always seeing you and never forsaking you.

DAY FIVE: COMPARE AND CONTRAST

Widow of Nain

Now that we've studied Hagar, let's compare her interaction with God to a New Testament woman in a similar situation. Though Hagar was only worried that her son was going to die, the widow of Nain's son was already dead when God came to her. We're all familiar with Lazarus's resurrection, but before Lazarus, Jesus restored to life an unnamed son of an obscure widow woman.

Jesus and his disciples were passing through Nain. They'd just come from Capernaum where Jesus had healed the centurion's servant. As they approached the city gate, they met a funeral procession heading to the burial grounds outside town. The deceased was the only son of a widow woman, and a large crowd was with her. Jesus saw the widow, felt compassion for her, and told her not to cry.

What an odd thing to say to a grieving mother at a funeral. Of course, she was crying. We'd be a little concerned if she wasn't upset. Jesus didn't stop there. He went to the coffin where her dead son rested. And then, to the surprise of all those watching, he brought a dead man back to life. By this time, Jesus had performed many miracles, but this was his first resurrection, and he did it so a nameless widow woman wouldn't be alone and forsaken.

Jesus was on an evangelistic journey to reach Galilee. He knew this woman needed him to come to her. He arranged his entrance through Nain's city gates to take place precisely when the funeral procession started.

This woman was at her depths. She'd already lost her husband. Now she'd lost her only son. She had no one to care for her in her remaining days. Feeling compassion for her suffering, Jesus performed a miracle for her.

Just as God saw Hagar, he saw the widow of Nain. Though the Bible doesn't tell us her name, Jesus knew who she was. He saw what she was going through, and he cared for her. He was there for her when it appeared her last hope was gone.

Opening Prayer

Pray for God to direct your time of Bible study.

Scripture Reading

Read the widow of Nain's story in Luke 7:11–18.

The widow of Nain, a woman like Hagar, is a New Testament account of a woman who was seen by God. Jesus saw her need and was there for her. Use your Bible reference tools to learn more. As you study the widow of Nain's story, compare and contrast her story to Hagar's story.

Listen to the *All God's Women* podcast episode or read the blog post on the widow of Nain.

Review Questions

How are Hagar and the widow of Nain alike?

What are the similarities between their stories?

What was the widow doing when Jesus came to her?

What did Jesus tell her to do?

What do both stories teach us about prayer?

What can you learn from the widow of the Nain's story?

When was a time in your life when everything looked hopeless but God intervened?

How does God use these experiences for his glory?

Scripture Memory Passage

Share Psalm 139:1–2 with others. You might choose to make a meme and share on social media along with a personal note. Better yet, find a way to incorporate the verse in an in-person conversation with a friend.

Closing Prayer

Ask God to open your eyes to other lessons you can learn from Hagar and the widow of Nain.

— Chapter Two —
Miriam

Miriam grew up in a godly home and witnessed firsthand the amazing power of God. She's the only Bible woman we follow through life from childhood to old age.

As a young girl, Miriam witnessed Pharaoh's attempts to kill Hebrew baby boys. She was there when Moses was born and overheard her parents' conversations, wondering what they would do to save their baby. For months, she had to keep silent about her family breaking the law. As a young girl with an active imagination, how Miriam must have worried as she helped rock Moses to sleep, fearful that at any moment soldiers might come and arrest them all for disobeying the law.

When her mom conceived the idea to put Moses in a basket and place him in the river, Miriam was there to keep an eye on him. I can picture Jochebed gently swaddling Moses in a blanket then wrapping her arm around Miriam and praying for safety and deliverance for her son.

Can you imagine their prayers of praise after Pharaoh's daughter rescued Moses and then offered to pay Jochebed to nurse him?

Miriam went on to witness God's wrath on the Egyptians through his plagues and followed his lead from enslavement in Egypt to freedom in the desert. As they embarked on their journey, she could see God's leading in a pillar of cloud by day and pillar of fire by night.

When the Egyptian army stormed behind them and the Red Sea blocked their passing, Miriam watched in amazement as Moses parted the sea and led millions of Hebrews across dry land to safety on the other side. She then watched as walls of water overtook mighty soldiers in their chariots. As bodies of dead soldiers washed up on the seashore, Miriam joined Moses in singing songs of praise then grabbed a tambourine and led all the women in their own time of praise and worship. Unfortunately, Miriam soon turned from praising to protesting.

DAY ONE: HER STORY

Moses married a Cushite, or Egyptian, woman. To show her displeasure, Miriam started whispered complaints about Moses. Then, as grumbling mounted, Aaron got involved. As an influential leader, Miriam stirred up discontent among her people, promoting her own self-importance and pointing out Moses wasn't the only prophet God spoke to. She tried dragging Moses down thinking this would lift her up. Her efforts didn't have the expected results.

God witnessed Miriam's activities and called the three siblings together for a meeting. He made clear to Miriam and Aaron that Moses was his chosen leader, and they should not speak out against him. The Lord left in a cloud, and when the cloud dissolved, Miriam was leprous.

For a woman in a public position, leprosy was the ultimate humiliation. Leprosy caused disfiguring skin sores, painful sensations, and deteriorating health. Since this disease was contagious, leprosy meant social isolation and disgrace.

As soon as Moses and Aaron saw what happened to Miriam, they begged and pleaded with God to heal her, and he did. He said for her to be shut out of the camp for seven days. This was her time of punishment and cleansing. After a week, God restored Miriam's health, so she was out of her discomfort and no longer an outcast.

God made his point with Miriam, but I love the verse that follows. Numbers 12:15 says, "So Miriam was shut outside the camp seven days, and the people did not set out on the march till Miriam was brought in again."

Despite Miriam's failures, the people loved her enough to tarry seven days until she could join them. At this point, they had no idea how long they would spend in the wilderness. They thought they were almost to their destination. Yet they were willing to wait a full week so Miriam could go with them. God wanted us to know, that though Miriam fell, she was not forgotten.

Opening Prayer

Pray that God will reveal truths to you through Miriam's story.

Scripture Reading

Read Numbers 12:1–16. As you read, place yourself in Miriam's place. Make note of God's treatment of Miriam, and what his treatment shows us about his character.

Review Questions

Why did Miriam complain about Moses?

What did Miriam say to the other women?

How did God respond to Miriam and Aaron's complaints against Moses?

Where did God meet with the three siblings?

What did God do to get Miriam's attention?

How did her brothers respond?

What was God's punishment for Miriam?

How did the people respond to Miriam's punishment?

Scripture Memory Passage

> Let no corrupting talk come out of your mouths, but only such as is good for building up, as fits the occasion, that it may give grace to those who hear. (Ephesians 4:29)

Read Ephesians 4:29 aloud. How does it relate to Miriam's story?

Closing Prayer

Replace "your mouths" with "my mouth" and recite Ephesians 4:29 as a prayer to God.

DAY TWO: HER STORY IN CONTEXT

Miriam was the first Bible woman named as a prophet. Being a prophet meant God spoke directly to her and through her. Because she was already called a prophetess when the Hebrews made their way out of Egypt, we can assume she'd been leading other women for quite some time. Miriam was the first women's ministry director and even had her own women's praise team.

When I used to read about Miriam rejoicing on the shores of the Red Sea, I always pictured her as a young woman caught up in the moment and celebrating in a wild, abandoned way, but she was an eighty-year-old woman at that time. She'd experienced a lot of life and more than her fair share of suffering. However, in this moment of rejoicing in God's goodness, she lost her inhibitions and focused on him. Miriam rejoiced in hope.

As the Israelites continued toward their promised land, Miriam witnessed daily miracles of manna and quail from heaven and water appearing where there wasn't any before. But something happened to Miriam. She became prideful, which caused her to grow jealous of her younger brother.

After her confrontation with God, we don't hear of Miriam again until her death. Some say she lost her prophetic abilities after God's judgment. I don't think so. Numbers 12:14 tells us, "Let her be shut outside the camp seven days, and after that she may be brought in again." Had God departed from her, he would have mentioned it. Instead, he made sure everyone knew she was to be welcomed back within the company.

I'd speculate that Miriam was forever changed after her encounter with God. She'd seen his power and felt his wrath. She'd also experienced God's mercy and grace. I suspect Miriam was a subdued woman going forward, not trying to lead the masses, but perhaps ministering one on one, showing compassion to those who were hurting, and warning those who were going astray.

Miriam knew God. She knew him in good times and bad. Don't you love that God made sure to let us know that the people waited for her? Though she'd failed big time, he'd not forgotten her, and neither had her people.

The Bible records Miriam's death in Kadesh before they entered Canaan. Though Scripture doesn't mention this, tradition indicates the people mourned thirty days for her. Is that true? We don't know, but based on their earlier behavior, their mourning makes sense.

Opening Prayer

Thank God for His goodness and mercy when you don't deserve it.

Scripture Reading

Read Exodus 15:20–21 and Numbers 20:1.

Additional reading: Genesis 16; 17:1–7.

How often do we go through mountaintop experiences of seeing God at work, only to lose sight of who he is and become consumed with our own importance? As you read the events leading up to Miriam's fall from grace, consider why she might have felt envious of Moses and needed to put him in his place.

Review Questions

How old was Miriam when they crossed the Red Sea?

How did Miriam respond to God bringing them to safety?

What influence did she have on other women?

What miracles did Miriam witness?

What was Miriam's role?

What was Moses's role?

Why might Miriam have felt superior to Moses?

What motivated Miriam's actions?

Scripture Memory Passage

Write Ephesians 4:29 on an index card. Tape it to your refrigerator door or wherever you will see it throughout the day.

Closing Prayer

Thank God specifically for blessings in your life.

DAY THREE: DIG DEEPER

The Bible gives us two examples of Miriam's interactions with God. The first is when she praised God for delivering them from Egypt. Miriam grabbed a timbrel, danced around, and celebrated God's goodness in bringing them out of Egypt.

Miriam's joy didn't last, though. She grew bitter and angry, sharing her thoughts with anyone who would listen. Just as God saw Hagar *in* trouble, he saw Miriam *causing* trouble. He was not pleased.

God ordered Miriam and her brothers to gather at the tabernacle of meeting. He came down in a pillar of cloud and called Miriam and Aaron forward, then explained why their complaints were out of line.

Numbers 12:9 tells us that the anger of the Lord was aroused against Miriam, and he struck her with leprosy. Fortunately, he also showed mercy on her, healing her leprosy. He gave her seven days in isolation to consider what she'd done, then allowed her to go on with her life.

In Miriam's life, we get to witness the heights and depths of walking with God. We see her rejoicing in his goodness and then rejecting his authority. Through her interactions with God, we witness his glory and his mercy.

Opening Prayer

Ask God to open your eyes to bad attitudes you may not realize.

Scripture Reading

Read Numbers 12:1–16 in at least one other Bible translation. As you read, make note of the cause-and-effect sequence between Miriam, her brothers, and God. See the flow chart on the next page to help you visualize the sequence.

MIRIAM AND GOD

What did Moses do? (v. 1)

↓

What did Miriam do as a result of what Moses did? (vv. 1–2)

↓

How did God react to what Miriam did? (v. 4)

↓

How did Miriam respond to God's command? (vv. 4–5)

↓

What did God say to Miriam and her brothers?)vv. 6–8)

↓

What did God do to Miriam? (v. 10)

↓

How did Aaron respond when he saw what God did to Miriam?
(vv. 11–12)

↓

How did Moses respond to Aaron's plea? (v. 13)

↓

How did the Lord respond to Moses's petition? (v. 14)

↓

What was Miriam's punishment (v. 15)

↓

How did the people respond to Miriam's punishment? (v. 15)

Review Questions

As we dig deeper into Miriam's story, we look at questions that aren't answered directly in the Bible but provide reflection to help better understand the situation.

Why did God punish Miriam and not Aaron?

How did God appear to the three siblings?

Why was God angry with what Miriam had done?

What was the difference between Miriam's attitude and Moses's attitude?

Why did God make her isolate for seven days?

How might Miriam's experience have changed her?

Why did the people wait for her?

How might Miriam have been changed as a result of her encounter with God?

Scripture Memory Passage

Every time you go to the refrigerator, recite Ephesians 4:29.

Closing Prayer

Pray for forgiveness for times when you speak against other people, judging them unfairly.

DAY FOUR: MAKE IT PERSONAL

Of all the women in the Bible, I am most like Miriam. I praise big and I fall hard. When I fail, I usually do so in a big way where everyone can see it. I am so thankful God forgives and forgets. He allows us to move on, and when we do, we are not the same women. We mellow through our failures. We hopefully grow wiser. We become vessels God uses to guide others who are going down similar paths. What an awesome God we serve who can take our failures and use them as our ministry.

For those of us who grew up in church, our failures are often initiated when we do what we think is right. In her mind, Miriam was righteous. Committed to the law of God about who Hebrews should marry, she was trying to keep Moses accountable. What she failed to factor in, however, was it was not her place to judge Moses. She appointed herself as his moral compass, when Moses's marriage choice was between him and God. God was able to see the heart of Moses. If he didn't have a problem with Moses marrying a Cushite woman, then who was Miriam to condemn him?

Our biggest failures often come on the heels of our greatest successes. The enemy knows to attack us at those moments because we're least expecting it.

As you read about Miriam, may you see yourself in her situation. Think about times when you've rejoiced and worshipped God with all your being. Reflect on examples in your life when you've witnessed God's miraculous hand at work, performing amazing miracles that defy understanding. Ponder situations when you allowed your pride to take over and potentially jeopardize your testimony. Thank God for loving you enough to discipline, then praise him for showing mercy and grace rather than the punishment you deserved.

Opening Prayer

Pray for God to search your heart and create in you a pure heart.

Scripture Study

Miriam is a fascinating woman to study, and so many resources are available on her. Enjoy discovering what others have said about her. Here are some suggestions for studying Miriam.

- Use a study Bible and read the notes about Miriam and her interactions with God.
- Read a commentary or sermon on Numbers 12:1–16. Make notes of anything that jumps out.
- Read about Miriam in a book about women in the Bible. So many books include her as an example to study.
- Listen to the *All God's Women* podcast episodes or read the blog posts on Miriam.
- Search for other blog posts or podcasts about Miriam.

To better understand God's character, it helps to get to know him by his different names. See a list of a few of his names in the Appendixes. Which names apply to Miriam's interactions with God? Which names do you connect with? Can you think of times when you experienced the different aspects of God's character?

Review Questions

What does the name Miriam mean?

How are you like Miriam?

When have you grown bitter in your life?

When have you felt prideful and looked down on the perceived sins of others?

How often have you complained about church leadership, wishing they did things your way?

Have you ever felt morally superior to someone God has placed over you?

Has there been a time when you deserved judgment but God showed you mercy?

How do you respond when God chastises you?

When was the last time you praised God with your whole being?

Scripture Memory Passage

Read aloud the memory passage then close your eyes or turn away and try saying it by memory. Can you do it yet?

Closing Prayer

Thank God for His tender mercies when you mess up.

DAY FIVE: COMPARE AND CONTRAST

Eve

Miriam had to face God after sinning. Eve was another woman who had to face him. Like Miriam, Eve witnessed firsthand bountiful blessings from God. Also like Miriam, she got caught up in her own wisdom. When the serpent told Eve she could be like God, she liked the idea. Who wouldn't want to be like God? In her mind, being like God made perfect sense.

Eve's downfall started with a question. The serpent asked Eve if God had indeed told them they could not eat from every tree in the garden. She confirmed they could eat from all of them except one, the Tree of the Knowledge of Good and Evil. Eve added an additional caveat—God had told them they couldn't touch or eat from the tree or else they'd die. God had only said not to eat from the tree. He hadn't mentioned touching.

The serpent played on Eve's weakness. He claimed to have a better understanding of God, explaining to her that God's reason for placing limits on what they could eat was to keep them from becoming as wise as him.

Like Miriam, Eve grew prideful. Not content with her place in life, Eve wanted to be as wise as God, knowing good from evil. After taking the first bite, she handed Adam his own piece of fruit, so they transgressed together.

The serpent was right. Once they ate from the tree, they knew good and evil. They understood what they'd had was good, and what they'd done was evil. They tried to cover up their sin. They tried to hide from God, but we all know we can't hide from God.

God called Eve and Adam out and delivered their punishment. The price Eve paid was high, but God didn't forsake her. He showed mercy and grace, allowing her to bear children and to be the mother of humankind.

Like Miriam, Eve sinned. God confronted her. God condemned her. God showed mercy on her.

Opening Prayer

Pray for God to give you discernment to recognize what is right and wrong.

Scripture Reading

Read God's confrontation with Eve in the garden of Eden in Genesis 3:1–24. As you read, make note of the similarities between Miriam's and Eve's interactions with God. Create your own cause-and-effect chart for Genesis 3 like we did with Miriam and God.

Listen to the *All God's Women* podcast episodes or read the blog posts on Eve.

Review Questions

How are Miriam and Eve alike?

What are the similarities between their stories?

How did God's treatment of the women compare?

How did the women react to God's judgment?

How did God show both judgment and mercy?

What impact did their actions have on the rest of their lives?

How are our lives impacted by our sins?

Scripture Memory Passage

Say the Scripture over and over until you can recite it from memory.

Closing Prayer

Ask God for forgiveness for those times when you get caught up in your own wisdom. Thank him for his mercy.

—Chapter Three—
Daughters of Zelophehad

Chances are, even if you've read the Bible through, you likely glossed over the five daughters of Zelophehad, and yet, they are a beautiful example of taking our petitions to God.

We're first introduced to the sisters in Numbers 26:33. "Now Zelophehad the son of Hepher had no sons, but daughters. And the names of the daughters of Zelophehad were Mahlah, Noah, Hoglah, Milcah, and Tirzah."

As Israel prepared to enter Canaan, God instructed Moses to take a second census. They'd conducted one when they departed Egypt, but this was a new generation. They needed to know how many men of fighting age they had who were able to go to war for Israel. The census was also used to determine distribution of land. Each tribe received a land grant which was divided among the families.

Numbers 26 contains the census results. Tucked away in the list of sons is inclusion of Zelophehad's daughters. You might easily skim over verse thirty-three without thinking much of it, but this verse foreshadows our need to be aware of these sisters.

Mahlah, Noah, Hoglah, Milcah, and Tirzah saw a problem. When everyone settled in Canaan, their family wouldn't be represented. Because they had no brother, they would have no land.

While men often had only daughters and no sons, up to this point no provision was made for the daughters. The assumption was that all women would marry and didn't need an inheritance of their own. The daughters of Zelophehad decided something needed to be done to provide for women. Their courage in addressing an unfair situation resulted in the creation of property laws for women.

DAY ONE: THEIR STORY

The daughters of Zelophehad had a problem. They also had a solution, but they had to go before Moses, Eleazar the priest, and congregational leaders. What they were proposing was unprecedented. They were asking for women's property rights.

The five women went together to the doorway of the tabernacle of meeting and presented their case. They focused not on themselves, but on their father.

They explained their father had died in the wilderness but was not part of any revolt against God. They asked, "Why should the name of our father be taken away from his clan because he had no son? Give to us a possession among our father's brothers" (Numbers 27:4).

The men listened to what the sisters had to say, then Moses took their petition to God.

God confirmed the women's request, giving Moses new property inheritance laws which Moses put into practice. These new laws allowed that if a man died with daughters but no sons, then his inheritance would pass to his daughters.

Because of five courageous sisters, all of Israel saw God's care and compassion for women, and a new precedence was set for women's rights.

Opening Prayer

Ask God to prepare your heart to learn from the daughters of Zelophehad's actions.

Scripture Reading

Read Numbers 26:33 and 27:1–11. As you read, make note of how the women approached their problem. What did they do? What did they not do?

Review Questions

What family did Zelophehad come from?

What were the names of the five daughters?

What was the daughters' problem?

How did they solve it?

How did they approach Moses?

What was their argument for their case?

How did Moses handle their request?

What was God's response?

Scripture Memory Passage

> If you remain in me, and my words remain in you, ask whatever you wish, and it will be done for you. (John 15:7)

Read aloud John 15:7. Relate this verse to the story of the daughters of Zelophehad, How did the girls remain in God? Why does God clarify that he answers our prayers if we abide in him?

Closing Prayer

Ask God to show you what it means to remain in him so you can ask him whatever you wish.

DAY TWO: THEIR STORY IN CONTEXT

The daughters of Zelophehad thought their problem was solved, but it wasn't quite yet.

> The heads of the fathers' houses of the clan of the people of Gilead the son of Machir, son of Manasseh, from the clans of the people of Joseph, came near and spoke before Moses and before the chiefs, the heads of the fathers' houses of the people of Israel. (Numbers 36:1)

As you'll recall from yesterday's reading, these were men who would be directly affected by the new inheritance laws. The daughters of Zelophehad would receive property that would have gone to them. They came to Moses complaining that they were fine with the daughters inheriting their father's portion, but what happened if they went on to marry outside their tribe? In that case, their inheritance would go to another tribe and their tribe's total inheritance would be reduced.

Moses agreed they had a valid concern. He added an amendment to his ruling to clarify that, for the daughters to inherit their father's property, they must marry within their tribe. They could marry whoever they wanted, but if they married into another tribe, they would lose their inheritance.

The women agreed. They each went on to marry men in the tribe of Joseph.

This settlement took place in the plains of Moab by the Jordan, across from Jericho, but as we know, Moses died before they crossed over the Jordan, and Joshua became their leader. Once they arrived in Canaan, and the tribes prepared to settle in their given lands, the girls went to Eleazar, Joshua, and the rulers, reminding them of Moses's ruling, giving them their father's inheritance. They received their property along with the men.

Opening Prayer

Ask God to guide you in important life decisions and to give you the courage to pursue what he's given you.

Scripture Reading

Read Numbers 36:1–12 and Joshua 17:1–6. Try not to get bogged down in the names and details but focus on the girls' petition and God's response to them.

Review

As you read today's Scripture, consider the situation from both the girls' point of view and the men's point of view.

Who complained about the women's property rights?

How did the men approach Moses?

What was their concern?

Why was Moses's decision a problem?

What did Moses do?

What restrictions did the women have in who they married?

Who were they allowed to marry?

How did the daughters of Zelophehad respond?

Why did the daughters of Zelophehad follow up?

What might have happened had they not followed up?

Scripture Memory Passage

Write John 15:7 on an index card. Say it aloud multiple times, placing emphasis on a different word each time. The first time, stress "if." The next time, "you." Continue with "remain" and other words in the sentence.

Closing Prayer

Pray that God will give you an understanding heart so when someone challenges you, you will respond with grace and dignity rather than getting upset.

DAY THREE: DIG DEEPER

The daughters of Zelophehad had no way to communicate personally with God. Instead, they took their issue to God's chosen leader, Moses, and he took it to God. God confirmed to Moses that their request should be granted. Later, family leaders questioned their petition, so Moses created stipulations they needed to obey.

Then the time came for the Israelites to enter their promised land. Moses had died. Joshua was now in charge. The women wanted to make sure he remembered their case. They reminded Joshua and the leaders they were entitled to an inheritance, and Joshua granted them their land.

Though they never talked directly with God, he heard their petition and spoke in their favor to Moses. The women agreed to Moses's conditions. When Moses died, they made sure Joshua remembered what God had told Moses.

God knows our hearts. He knew the daughters of Zelophehad were not thinking only of themselves. He knew they were watching out for other women who found themselves in the same situation. He granted their request because of his compassion for women who were often overlooked or taken advantage of by men.

Opening Prayer

Pray that God would open your eyes to ways that you might be used to impact the lives of others.

Scripture Study

Read Numbers 27:1–11 and 36:1–12 in a different version of the Bible.

Use a study Bible or commentary to research the Scripture passage.

Review Questions

What was the motive of the daughters of Zelophehad?

How did they approach the leaders?

Why did they follow up?

How did their petition impact future generations?

Do you think they faced resistance from resentful men?

Based on what we know about the women, how might they have handled the resentment?

Scripture Memory Passage

Read aloud John 15:7, placing special emphasis on the first half of the sentence.

Closing Prayer

Pray for a specific need you have, checking your heart to make sure your motives are in line with the Lord.

DAY FOUR: MAKE IT PERSONAL

The daughters of Zelophehad must have worried about what would become of them in the promised land. With no men in their family, they would have no land. As they pondered their situation, they developed a solution, but it was so big, would it even be considered?

The daughters of Zelophehad could have taken the easy way out and married. That way they'd be provided for, and they wouldn't have to worry about an inheritance. But these sisters were seeking a long-term solution for generations of women to come, some of whom might never marry. They were fighting for the rights of women who might not have a voice. They wanted to impact lives long after they were dead.

What these five sisters asked for was unprecedented. They had no idea how Moses might respond to their revolutionary request, but they took a risk which paid off.

Have you ever had a dream so big it scared you? What did you do? So often we dismiss dreams because we're afraid to ask. The magnitude of our aspiration overwhelms us, so we do nothing. But what if God has given you this vision because he wants to use you to impact the lives of others?

If you have a deep desire, search your heart for motive. Once you're assured your heart is right, ask God to grant your request, even if a positive reply seems impossible. Worst case scenario, he says no. Best case, he uses you as an instrument of change that will continue blessing others long after you're gone.

Opening Prayer

Think about a recent prayer request. Take it to God, asking him to reveal to you if your petition is of him or of you.

Scripture Study

To fully appreciate the significance of the daughters of Zelophehad's petition, we need to understand their culture and laws.

- Use a Bible dictionary, other reference books, or online resources to research Old Testament property and inheritance laws and/or women's rights during the Old Testament era. An interesting side study might be to compare rights of women granted by God compared to rights of women given in other religions.
- In addition to your Scripture study, check out "And Zelophehad had Daughters," an article by Henry C. Clay, published in the February 1924 issue of American Bar Association Journal, pages 133–134. The article provides an interesting look at the biblical judgment from a legal perspective and is available online at https://www.jstor.org/stable/25711523?seq=1.
- Listen to the All God's Women podcast episode or read the blog post on Daughters of Zelophehad.

Review Questions

What can you learn from the daughters of Zelophehad's story?

How did God react to their request?

What does this tell us about God's character?

What does this tell us about how God feels about women?

Do you think the women expected God to respond as he did?

Do you think the women made the request lightly or did they put a lot of thought into it?

Do you think they expected Moses to respond as he did?

Have you ever had a prayer request so big you were afraid to pray?

Have you ever had an answered prayer that caught you by surprise because you weren't expecting God to answer the way he did?

Do you ever pray for something then later realize what a selfish or foolish request it was?

Do your prayers affect others or are your prayers focused solely on yourself?

Scripture Memory Passage

Write John 15:7 on a piece of paper. Underneath, list prayer requests. Read aloud the verse and the prayer requests.

Closing Prayer

Pray for the requests on your list, asking God to confirm the ones which are his desires and not only yours.

DAY FIVE: COMPARE AND CONTRAST

Salome

The daughters of Zelophehad had a major petition. So did Salome in the New Testament, but unlike the five sisters, Salome didn't think through her motivation nor the consequences of her request.

Salome was the wife of Zebedee and the mother of James and John. She was a devoted wife and mother as well as a follower of Jesus. She was one of a group of women who traveled with Jesus and his disciples, helping provide financially for them.

We're first introduced to Salome in Matthew 20. Jesus and his disciples and followers are traveling to Jerusalem, and Jesus is preparing them for what is to come in the days ahead. He warns them how he'll be betrayed and killed and rise again. In the middle of Jesus's deep discussion, Salome blurts out a request for her sons. She kneels with her sons and says she wants to ask him something. He asks what she wants, and she asks if her sons can sit one on each side next to him when he sets up his kingdom.

What an audacious selfish ask at such an inopportune time. Salome wanted the best for her sons, but rather than prayerfully considering her request and approaching Jesus at a proper time in an appropriate manner, she interrupted Jesus's spiritual teaching to request special treatment for her sons. Even if her petition had been acceptable, she went about it wrong.

Jesus's response shows how little she and her sons understood what she was asking. However, Jesus, in his graciousness and mercy, used the opportunity to continue teaching them what they could expect.

Opening Prayer

Pray for God's discernment to guide you in knowing what to pray for.

Scripture Reading

Read Salome's story in Matthew 20:20–24.

Compare the requests from the daughters of Zelophehad and Salome. Create your own chart showing similarities and differences in their requests and how they asked for their requests. Include their requests, how much thought went into them, how they presented their petitions, God's response to their request, and how they dealt with God's response.

Listen to the All God's Women podcast episode or read the blog post on Salome.

Review Questions

How are Salome and the daughters of Zelophehad alike?

How are their requests similar?

How are their requests different?

How did their motives differ?

How did their timing compare?

How did God's response to their requests differ?

Why did God answer the daughters' request but deny Salome's?

What can we learn from God's response to their requests?

Scripture Memory Passage

Consider the memory passage whenever you're asking requests from God.

Closing Prayer

Ask for forgiveness for those times when you get greedy and ask for things outside of God's will.

—Chapter Four—
Deborah

If you're looking for an uplifting read, the book of Judges is probably not for you. Covering an era much like modern days, Judges is a gory book filled with vile behaviors. But amid unbelievable corruption and violence, a housewife named Deborah shined light in the darkness.

Deborah was an unassuming woman, married to an obscure man. She was a prophetess, which means she communed with God. He spoke to her. She listened. And she shared what he said to those around her. God chose her to lead her people as judge of the land.

Deborah did not seek a leadership position. She stayed at home, talking and listening to God, and he sent the people to her front yard. Though Deborah served God in a humble way, he used her in a mighty way. When God said to speak, she spoke. When he said to go, she went. When he said to lead, she led. When those around her were timid and afraid, Deborah was bold and brave. And when God performed a mighty victory for the Israelites, Deborah was the first to give him all praise and glory.

Under normal circumstances, God would probably not have chosen a woman to lead his people, but these were not normal times. In a time of uncontrolled chaos, God worked in a most unexpected manner to get the attention of his people. Her weakness as a humble woman brought to light God's strength. People recognized that Deborah was only a vessel used by God. He was her source of power.

DAY ONE: HER STORY

Deborah spent her days under a palm tree in her front yard, and the children of Israel came to her for wisdom and judgment.

One man who didn't come to Deborah for advice was Barak, the son of Abinoam from Kedesh in Naphtali. God gave Deborah a message for Barak, but she knew God had already given the command to Barak directly. Since he didn't respond to God's command, she confronted Barak.

Judges 4:6–7 tells us:

> She sent and summoned Barak the son of Abinoam from Kedesh-naphtali and said to him, "Has not the LORD God of Israel, commanded you, 'Go, gather your men at Mount Tabor, taking 10,000 from the people of Naphtali and the people of Zebulun. And I will draw out Sisera, the general of Jabin's army, to meet you by the river Kishon with his chariots and his troops, and I will give him into your hand'?"

She wasn't giving Barak a new command. She was merely confirming what he'd already been told. Only he was scared.

His response? He said the only way he'd go was if Deborah went with him. Imagine how far Israel had fallen that a military leader would only go to battle if a woman went with him.

She agreed to go with him, but she warned him that, because of his refusal to go without her, a woman would get the glory for defeating Sisera.

Deborah was not a militant woman, but she left the comfort of her home in the mountains of Ephraim to accompany Barak and his army to Kedesh, some seventy miles away.

Ten thousand Israelite soldiers on foot were no match for Sisera's mighty army and chariots, but they huddled on the mountain and waited for their next command.

At the appointed time, Deborah told Barak, "Up! For this is the day in which the LORD has given Sisera into your hand. Does not the LORD go out before you?" (Judges 4:14). Barak listened to her words and went down from the mountain with his ten thousand men following him.

We learn from Deborah's song of praise in Judges 5 that as the Israelite warriors made their way down Mount Tabor, God sent a massive storm. Sisera's army was situated in the dry riverbed of the Kishon, but the torrential downpour blinded them and the floodwaters overflowed the river banks. Sisera's heavy chariots got trapped in mud, forcing his soldiers to flee on foot. They made easy targets for the Hebrew army, with everyone dying by the sword except for Sisera. Sisera, however, met his match with Jael, another homemaker, who undertook the gruesome task of bringing him to his death. Jael was the woman Deborah prophesied would get the glory for defeating Sisera.

Opening Prayer

When you pray, remember to not only talk to God, but spend time listening as well.

Scripture Reading

Read Judges 4–5. As you read, make note of the difference between Deborah and those around her.

Review Questions

What type of woman was Deborah?

Who was her husband?

Where did Deborah live?

What did she do under the palm tree?

Why did she go to Barak?

What was Barak's condition to fight Sisera's army?

What did Deborah tell Barak would happen after the battle?

What did Deborah do once the troops were in place?

How did the battle end?

What did Deborah do after the Hebrew victory?

Scripture Memory Passage

> If any of you lacks wisdom, let him ask God, who gives generously to all without reproach, and it will be given him. (James 1:5)

Read aloud James 1:5. How does it apply to Deborah's story?

Closing Prayer

Ask God to give you wisdom in all that you do.

DAY TWO: HER STORY IN CONTEXT

The book of Judges opens with Joshua's death and explains how Israel failed to follow God's instructions to defeat their enemies. Instead, God's people chose to intermarry and intertwine with the pagans. They lost sight of who they were, and God allowed them to become oppressed by their enemies.

For over two hundred years, the children of Israel followed a pattern. They did evil in the sight of the Lord. He gave them over to their enemies. They cried out to God for mercy. He raised up judges to deliver them, and, as long as they listened to the judges, they experienced times of peace. But once a judge died, they'd go back to their old ways, behaving even more corruptly than before.

In Judges chapter 4, the Israelites were held captive by Jabin, king of Canaan. Sisera, his army commander, harshly oppressed the Israelites for twenty years.

Sisera's army used their nine hundred iron chariots to terrorize travelers on roadways between towns. As a result, Israelites were forced to hide in the hills and travel backroads where chariots couldn't reach. Village life was almost completely wiped out. Israelites lived in constant fear. This was the world Deborah lived in.

Opening Prayer

Pray for God to reveal to you how the Israelite situation during Deborah's time relates to your life today.

Scripture Reading

Read Judges 1–2. What does it tell us about the state of Israel and the world Deborah lived in?

Review Questions

Who did the Israelites fight against?

What did Manasseh not do?

Why was there a problem when Israel didn't drive out all the Canaanites?

What did God tell his people would happen as a result of their failure to follow his commands?

How did the Israelites respond to God's judgment on them?

What happened to the generation of Israelites after Joshua died?

Who did the Israelites begin worshipping?

Did people listen to the judges?

What happened when the judges died?

Bonus question:

Tucked away in Judges 1 is a story of women and property rights. Did you spot it?

Scripture Memory Passage

Write James 1:5 on an index card. Use the index card as a bookmark inside your favorite Bible.

Closing Prayer

Pray for God to reveal to you any ways that you're compromising your faith.

DAY THREE: DIG DEEPER

Deborah celebrated the defeat of Sisera's army by praising God. Judges 5 is her song of praise. In one of the oldest poems in the Bible, Deborah, depicts life for Israel during their dark days and how God rescued them. She opened and closed her song celebrating God and his power to protect his people.

> That the leaders took the lead in Israel,
> that the people offered themselves willingly,
> bless the LORD!
> Hear, O kings;
> give ear, O princes;
> to the LORD I will sing;
> I will make melody to the LORD, the God of Israel.
> (Judges 5:2–3)
> So may all your enemies perish, O LORD!
> But your friends be like the sun as he rises in his might."
> (Judges 5:31)

Not only does Deborah praise God in Judges 5, but she paints a vivid picture of all that Israel was dealing with and the details of how God saved them from the oppression of Sisera.

Opening Prayer

Praise God for what he is doing and has done in your life.

Scripture Reading

Read Judges 5 in multiple Bible translations.

Look up the Hebrew translations for verses dealing with God and his people.

Review Questions

What does Deborah's song reveal about life for the Israelites?

How many ways did God reveal himself to the Israelites?

How did the earth respond to God?

How does Deborah describe herself?

What does Deborah say about Jael?

What does she say about Sisera's mother?

How does chapter 5 close?

Scripture Memory Passage

Every time you open your Bible, read aloud James 1:5 from your index card bookmark.

Closing Prayer

Think of a specific decision you're pondering. Ask God to give you wisdom as you make the decision.

DAY FOUR: MAKE IT PERSONAL

Deborah was a homemaker. Though she called herself "a mother in Israel" (Judges 5:7), we have no indication that she had children of her own. Instead, she is referring to herself as mothering the children of Israel.

The Israelite world that Deborah lived in was a place where people desperately needed someone to mother them. They lived in fear, oppressed by their enemies, and surrounded by violence. They needed someone to go to who would encourage and guide them, to let them know that everything was going to be all right. Deborah became that person.

Deborah probably would have rather remained at home under her palm tree than to travel across the country and lead army troops to battle. But when faced with the challenge, she demonstrated her faith by following God outside her comfort zone. Her faith was contagious. The men listened to her because they knew she walked with God and her walk was real. Because of her, they were victorious.

Our world today is much like the Israelite world during the time of Deborah and the other judges. Deborah was surrounded by people who'd lost sight of God, compromised their faith, and now were suffering the consequences. Isn't that very much how we're living today? We, as a society, have lost sight of God as we've pursued our own selfish beliefs. We've compromised our faith in our attempts to be more palatable to our enemies. We're suffering the consequences of lukewarm Christianity.

We need to take lessons from Deborah, learning to be bold and brave, unafraid to do and say the right thing, and to follow God wherever he leads us despite the dangers.

Opening Prayer

Ask God to help you step out of your comfort zone and follow him however he leads.

Scripture Study

Choose one of these options to study Judges 5 more in-depth. Whichever study method you choose, make notes of what your research reveals about Deborah and what it reveals about God. You may want to make a chart to sort the revelations.

- Read at least one sermon on Deborah's song.
- Use a study Bible or commentary to help you understand Deborah's song and all that it reveals about Israel, her oppressors, their battles, and their victory.
- Look up Judges 5 in the original language. Does it reveal anything new?
- Make a chart with a column for the Israelites and a column for the Canaanites. In each column jot down descriptive words and phrases included in Judges 5.
- Listen to the All God's Women podcast episode or read the blog post on Deborah.

Review Questions

What is the significance of Deborah's story in the Bible?

How are you like Deborah?

How are you different from Deborah?

What can you learn from Deborah's story?

How did God use Deborah?

What did Deborah know about God's character?

How can you find encouragement in Deborah's story?

Which characteristics of God do we see in Deborah's story?

When was the last time you listened to God speak to you?

What is God asking you to do right now?

Are you willing to do whatever God asks of you?

Scripture Memory Passage

Read aloud James 1:5 over and over until you can say it by memory.

Closing Prayer

Spend time in silence seeking wisdom from the Lord.

DAY FIVE: COMPARE AND CONTRAST

Manoah's Wife

Deborah wasn't the only humble woman married to an obscure man who heard from God. The Angel of the Lord appeared to Manoah's wife and told her she would conceive a son. Then he gave her specific instructions for what to do during her pregnancy. She was not to drink any alcoholic beverages or eat anything unclean. And when the child was born, she was never to cut his hair because he would be a Nazarite to God from birth.

With an amazing display of faith, Manoah's wife didn't question the angel in any way, but rather immediately ran to tell her husband the good news.

Manoah wasn't convinced. He and his wife were undistinguished, unknown Israelites from the family of Dan, certainly not worthy of a personal visit from God. His wife so desperately wanted a child—she surely just imagined the whole thing.

But he prayed and asked the Lord to come again and teach them what they should do for the son who was to be born.

God listened to his prayer and the angel came again to Mrs. Manoah. She was alone in the fields, but she ran quickly to her husband and dragged him to the angel. He heard for himself what the angel had already told his wife.

Manoah's wife did give birth to a son, and she named him Samson, which means "strength of the sun." We're told that Samson grew and the Lord blessed him (Judges 13:24).

Opening Prayer

Ask God to open your heart so you hear him whenever he speaks to you.

Scripture Reading

Read Manoah's wife's story in Judges 13. As you read the passage, note the similarities and differences between Deborah and Manoah's wife.

Listen to the All God's Women podcast episode or read the blog post on Manoah's wife.

Review Questions

How are Deborah and Manoah's wife alike?

What are the similarities between their stories?

Where was Manoah's wife when the Angel of the Lord came to her?

What did the angel tell her to do?

What do both stories teach us about prayer?

What do both stories teach us about obeying God?

What can you learn from Manoah's wife's story?

Have you ever received a word from God but others questioned whether it was really God who spoke to you?

How should we react when we hear from God?

Scripture Memory Passage

Share James 1:5 with at least one other person today, either in conversation with a loved one or friend or sharing on social media.

Closing Prayer

Thank God for any wisdom and discernment he's given you.

—Chapter Five—
Hannah

Of all the stories of women in the Bible, Hannah best illustrates a praying woman. A barren wife of a polygamist husband, taunted by her rival, discouraged by rampant corruption not only within Israel's general population, but among God's priests in his temple, Hannah could have blamed God for all that was wrong. Instead, she took her problems to him.

Hannah went to the temple, pouring out her soul to God, weeping bitterly with a broken heart over the sinfulness surrounding her. Though the situation looked hopeless, Hannah prayed for a miracle. She asked God for a son, but not just any son. Hannah asked for the privilege of bearing a child who would help lead his people back to their Lord. This was no ordinary prayer, but God heard her request. He knew her heart. He granted her appeal.

Hannah conceived a son and named him Samuel. When he was three years old, Hannah took him to the temple and left him there to serve the rest of his days as a man of God.

How hard it must have been hard to give up her baby boy, but as Hannah left the temple, she burst into prayer again, not in sorrow at saying goodbye, but in praise for the honor God had bestowed on her.

Though Hannah was content with what God had given her, God hadn't finished blessing her. He opened her womb so she bore three sons and two daughters.

Day One: Her Story

We meet Hannah in chapter one of First Samuel. She was married to Elkanah, a Levite who lived in Ramathaim Zophim. The first thing we learn about her is she was one of two wives, that the other wife had children and Hannah had none. Because Hannah's name is mentioned first, we can assume she was Elkanah's first wife, and because of her infertility, Elkanah took a second wife, Peninnah. Although he took care of Peninnah and her children, Hannah was his first love whom he loved the most.

Of course, as you can imagine, that didn't go over well with Peninnah. The Bible refers to her as Hannah's rival, and says she provoked Hannah severely to make her life miserable. Peninnah's attacks were especially harsh when the family made their annual trek to Shiloh to worship and sacrifice. Year after year, at a time when Hannah should be able to find peace with her Lord, she was antagonized to the point she would weep and not eat anything instead.

Poor Elkanah. He worried about his wife and tried to comfort her, asking her why she cried and why she wouldn't eat. "Am I not more to you than ten sons?" (1 Sam. 1:8).

Elkanah loved Hannah, but he didn't understand her. He didn't comprehend the anguish she felt.

No one else understood Hannah's sorrow, so she took her concerns to the only one who truly understood her misery. She left the family's table and went to the tabernacle where in bitterness of soul she poured out her heart to God. She wept in anguish and prayed for God to look down on her and remember her and give her a son, and then, she would give that son to God for all the days of his life.

Even when Hannah went to the temple to pray, she was misunderstood. Eli, the High Priest watched from his perch by the doorpost. He saw her crying and her lips moving but no sound coming forth and accused her of drinking. Used to worshippers merely going through the motions of prayer, when Eli witnessed Hannah's heartfelt prayers, he didn't recognize her behavior for what it was. He assumed she was drunk since that was more common.

Most of us would have been greatly insulted by the accusation, but Hannah was too caught up in her conversation with God to be offended. Hannah defended herself to Eli, and he acknowledged his mistake. He told her to "Go in peace, and the God of Israel grant your petition that you have made to him" (v. 17).

Once Hannah surrendered her burdens to God, they no longer weighed her down. She went back to her family restored and no longer sad. Even though God had yet to answer her prayer, her heart was at peace because she knew he had heard her prayers.

Early the next morning, the family went once more to the tabernacle to worship before returning home, but God "remembered" Hannah. She conceived and bore a son whom she called Samuel. She cherished her beloved son and nursed him until he was weaned. Then she took him to the temple and dedicated him to the Lord.

Opening Prayer

Pray for God to show you how to pray like Hannah.
Scripture Reading
Read 1 Samuel 1:1–29. As you read, make note of how others viewed Hannah and how God viewed Hannah.

Review Questions

Why was Hannah sad?

What compounded her grief?

What did Hannah pray for?

How did she feel after she prayed?

How did God answer Hannah's prayer?

What did Hannah do once her child was weaned?

How did God bless Hannah's faithfulness?

Scripture Memory Passage

> In my distress I called upon the LORD; to my God I cried for help. From his temple he heard my voice, and my cry to him reached his ears. (Psalm 18:6)

Read aloud Psalm 18:6. How does this passage relate to Hannah?

Closing Prayer

Rewrite Psalm 18:6 as a personal prayer.

DAY TWO: HER STORY IN CONTEXT

Hannah didn't just pray for a son. She made a bargain with God. If he gave her a son, she would dedicate that son and give him to the Lord. And she was a woman of her word. For three years she nursed and cared for Samuel, teaching him about the Lord, training him for what was ahead.

When the time came, and he was weaned. she took that little boy and presented him to Eli, the same priest who couldn't even recognize what soulful prayer looked like. She left her baby boy with Eli so he could serve God all the days of his life.

We're told in 1 Samuel 2:18 that even as a child, Samuel ministered before the Lord. Each year, Hannah and Elkanah came to visit him when they came to the temple to make their yearly sacrifice, and Hannah would make him a new linen robe. Eli blessed Hannah and Elkanah for giving their son to the Lord, and God opened Hannah's womb so she bore three sons and two daughters.

Though Samuel was raised in Eli's priestly home, growing up in the temple, he lived in a depraved environment. Eli's sons did not follow in their father's faith, instead, they used their priestly position for their own personal gratification. They stole from worshipers' meat sacrifices and took advantage of women who assembled at the door of the tabernacle of meeting. Their behavior grieved their father, but "... the boy Samuel continued to grow both in stature and in favor with the Lord and also with man" (1 Sam. 2:26).

Samuel's earliest days with Hannah gave him a foundation of faith. Her prayers helped him sustain that faith.

Samuel was a mere boy when God first spoke to him. He continued to hear directly from God throughout his life. He was the last of the Israelite judges, served as priest, and anointed kings. When he died, "... all Israel assembled and mourned for him ..." (1 Sam. 25:1).

Opening Prayer

Pray for your children and grandchildren (current and future) that God will instill in them a strong foundation to stand firm in whatever they face.

Scripture Reading

Read 1 Samuel 2. Note the contrast between Hannah and Samuel and those around them.

Review Questions

In Samuel's day, did men or women commonly hear directly from God?

What does Hannah reveal about herself in her prayer?

What does she say God does?

What kind of environment was Eli's home?

How did Hannah prepare her son a godly heritage?

How did Samuel contrast with Eli's sons?

Scripture Memory

Write out Psalm 18:6. Underneath, list what the psalmist did and how God responded.

Closing Prayer

Pray that you'll be able to hear the voice of God when he speaks to you.

DAY THREE: DIG DEEPER

Hannah didn't wait until after the Lord answered her prayer before rejoicing. Once she gave her request to the Lord, her face was no longer sad, and she eagerly worshipped God the next morning. Hannah and Elkanah returned home, and God answered her prayer by blessing her with a son. Hannah named that son Samuel because "I have asked for him from the LORD" (1 Sam. 1:20).

Oh, how easy it would have been for Hannah to forget her commitment to God, but no, she joyfully "lent" Samuel to the Lord all the days of his life. Hannah hadn't wanted a son merely to be a mother. She wasn't looking for vindication from Peninnah, nor just looking for a son to pass along a legacy. No, Hannah wanted a son who would bring revival to a hurting and lost land. She rejoiced in being allowed to bear a son who would prepare a path for change in the land.

After Hannah dedicated Samuel and left him with Eli at the temple, she prayed one of the most beautiful prayers in Scripture. The second chapter of First Samuel is a prayer of praise and prophecy and includes some of the earliest references to the coming Savior. Hannah saw wickedness overtaking the world and undertook Israel's need for redemption. She was honored and blessed to be used by God to bear a child who would help pave the way for the Savior of the world.

Scripture Reading

Read 1 Samuel 1:18–28 and 2:1–10 in multiple Bible versions. As you read, note what Hannah's prayer reveals to us about the character of God.

Review Questions

In Hannah's prayer, what does Hannah say that she does?

What advice does she give to others?

Why is Hannah rejoicing when she just gave up her child?

What does Hannah's prayer reveal about her relationship with God?

What does her prayer reveal about the world around her?

What does Hannah tell us about the character of God?

What does Hannah prophesy?

Scripture Memory

Read aloud Psalm 18:6 several times placing emphasis on the verbs.

Closing Prayer

Read aloud 1 Samuel 2:1–10 as your prayer.

DAY FOUR: MAKE IT PERSONAL

We tend to read stories like Hannah's and think that all we have to do is pray hard enough, and God will give us the desires of our heart. We have it wrong. We make out our shopping list of prayer requests and then wonder why God doesn't give us what we're asking for. We're missing the point of prayer.

Prayer is emptying ourselves and baring our soul to God, coming to him completely broken, not seeking selfish pleasures, but allowing him to open our eyes to what he wants for us. We truly start to see answered prayer when we give ourselves over to him and to his desires.

Hannah could have prayed for Peninnah to leave her alone. She could have prayed for revenge. She could have prayed for Elkanah to have a better understanding of her difficulties with Peninnah. She could have prayed for a quiver full of children to bring her joy all the days of her life.

Instead, Hannah shared her sorrows with God, then she prayed for the privilege of birthing a son who would change a nation. How could God not answer that prayer?

Opening Prayer

Ask God if what you're praying for is of him or of you.

Scripture Study

Pick apart Hannah's story. Select a passage from 1 Samuel 1–2 and zoom in on it.

- Look at Hannah's life and how she dealt with her problems.
- Analyze Hannah's prayer.
- Look at Hannah's marriage or her relationship with Samuel.

- Whatever aspect you choose, do a thorough study by researching study notes, Hebrew translations, sermons, or commentary.
- Listen to the All God's Women podcast episode or read the blog post on Hannah.
- Find other blogs and podcasts on Hannah.

Review Questions

What do you have in common with Hannah?

How are you different from Hannah?

What can you learn from Hannah's story?

What kind of relationship did Hannah have with God?

What did Hannah know about God's character?

How can you find encouragement in Hannah's story?

Depending on the Bible translation, Hannah refers to God by different names. What names does she call him?

How do your prayers compare with Hannah's?

Do you lay your burdens at God's feet?

Are you willing to do whatever God asks of you?

Scripture Memory

Write Psalm 18:6 in your own words.

Closing Prayer

Pour out your heart to God, then leave your sorrows with him.

DAY FIVE: COMPARE AND CONTRAST

Anna

We don't see a lot of Bible women spending time in the temple, but Luke tells us of a woman who spent most of her life in the temple.

Anna was a prophetess of the tribe of Asher. Her husband died after seven years of marriage, leaving her a widow until she was about eighty-four years old. She lived at the temple and served God twenty-four hours a day, so she was there when Mary and Joseph brought Jesus to Jerusalem for his baby dedication.

As Simeon held baby Jesus in his arms and proclaimed a blessing and prophecy over him, Anna entered the scene and witnessed for herself the young Christ child. "And coming up at that very hour she began to give thanks to God and to speak of him to all who were waiting for the redemption of Jerusalem" (Luke 2:38).

Opening Prayer

Pray that God will help you to remain faithful throughout your life so you might not ever miss the blessings he has in store for you.

Scripture Reading

Read Luke 2:22–38. Make note of similarities with Hannah.

Listen to the All God's Women podcast episode or read the blog post on Anna.

Review Questions

How are Hannah and Anna's stories alike?

How were both women faithful?

What do both stories teach us about prayer?

What can you learn from Anna's story?

Do you have prayers you've been praying for years without answer?

Have you had prayers God answered long after you'd lost hope?

Are you in place and ready for God's blessings?

Scripture Memory Passage

Try reciting Psalm 18:6 by memory. Recite it aloud to a family member or friend.

Closing Prayer

Thank God for answered prayers that came after a long time of waiting.

—Chapter Six—
Samaritan Woman

Tension rose between Jesus and the Pharisees. Jesus left Judea for Galilee because the time had not yet come for confrontation. The natural route between the two regions led through Samaria, but Jews and Samaritans were sworn enemies. Devout Jews usually went out of their way to avoid Samaria. Jesus felt no such need.

Jesus sat by a well while his disciples went in search of food. He should have been alone since it was midday, the hottest time of day.

Only he wasn't.

A lone woman came to draw water as Jesus rested and waited for the return of his disciples. Ignoring social norms that discouraged a man from addressing a woman in public, especially a stranger, and one who opposed Jews speaking to Samaritans, Jesus reached out to a woman who even the Samaritans dismissed due to her sordid reputation. He asked her for a drink of water.

The effect of that simple request was to have far-reaching consequences for the Samaritan community.

Jesus and his disciples didn't accidentally arrive in town at the exact time the Samaritan woman was drawing her water. He planned it. Though he asked her for a drink, their conversation had nothing to do with his thirst. He merely used his request to initiate a conversation with a woman condemned by the world. Jesus knew her past, but he saw in her a great future. He also saw in her the potential to impact and change the trajectory of those who knew her.

DAY ONE: HER STORY

We find the Samaritan woman's story in the Gospel of John, chapter 4. Jesus and his disciples were passing through Sychar in Samaria on their way from Judea to Galilee.

Though other women drew their water during early morning or evening hours, this woman came midday to avoid the interactions with and scorn of other women. She would have been surprised to see a Jewish man sitting at the well when she got there. She would have been shocked when he talked to her, asking her for a drink of water.

The woman asked him why he, a Jew, would ask her, a Samaritan woman, for a drink. She pointed out that Jews didn't associate with Samaritans.

Jesus responded, "If you knew the gift of God, and who it is that is saying to you, 'Give me a drink,' you would have asked him, and he would have given you living water" (John 4:10).

This confused the woman. What was this stranger talking about? He had no pot, no way to draw water. Where was this living water coming from?

Jesus explained that water from the well left you thirsty after a while, but the water he offered was a "a spring of water welling up to eternal life" (v.14). She wanted some of that water. Imagine not ever having to go to the well again.

Then Jesus told her to go get her husband and bring him to Jesus. The woman admitted she had no husband. Jesus affirmed her statement, revealing she'd had five husbands, and the man she was currently living with was not her husband. Imagine her shock to discover a Jewish man who knew about her sordid lifestyle and still made conversation with her, treating her with dignity rather than contempt.

The Samaritan woman recognized Jesus was no ordinary man. She judged he was a prophet, so she asked him where they should worship, pointing out the Jews believed it to be Jerusalem, while Samaritans worshipped on their mountain.

Jesus told her of things to come when their place of worship would not matter. He said soon all true worshipers would worship the Father in spirit and truth.

She responded, "I know that Messiah is coming (he who is called Christ). When he comes, he will tell us all things." (John 4:25). Though a Samaritan, she knew about the promised Messiah and trusted that when he came, he would answer her questions.

Then Jesus revealed himself to her. "I who speak to you am he." (John 4:26) With that simple statement, Jesus let her know he was her awaited Messiah.

At that moment, the disciples returned, and the woman left her waterpot and ran into town to share with her townspeople what had just happened.

Opening Prayer

Pray for God to direct your paths so you are where you need to be to meet with Jesus.

Scripture Reading

Read John 4:1–26. As you read, make note of all the reasons why the Samaritan woman should never have had an interaction with Jesus and all the things that could have happened to prevent her from receiving the gospel from Jesus.

Review Questions

Why did Jesus pass through Samaria?

Why was the woman at the well then?

Why was she the only woman getting water?

What did Jesus ask from the woman?

Did she give Jesus what he asked for?

What questions did she ask him?

How did she know Jesus was a prophet?

How did she know he was the Messiah?

What did she do as soon as she knew who he was?

Of all the people in Samaria, why did Jesus select this particular woman to talk to?

Scripture Memory Passage

> On the last day of the feast, the great day, Jesus stood up and cried out, "If anyone thirsts, let him come to me and drink. Whoever believes in me, as the Scripture has said, 'Out of his heart will flow rivers of living water.'" (John 7:37–38)

Read aloud John 7:37–38. How do these verses relate to the Samaritan woman?

Closing Prayer

Pray that God will open your heart so you're receptive to what he wants to teach you.

DAY TWO: HER STORY IN CONTEXT

The disciples returned from town and were surprised to see Jesus talking to the Samaritan woman, but they said nothing. She left behind her waterpot and hurried into town.

The Samaritan woman couldn't wait to share her experience with the men of the town. She told them about this man who must be the Christ. She invited them to come see for themselves.

Meanwhile, back at the well, Jesus's disciples tried to get him to eat, but he said he didn't need food, that he had food to eat which they didn't know about. He explained his food was to do the will of God.

Jesus explained to his disciples that the fields were ripe for harvest, and they were going to reap what others had labored for.

John 4:39–42 tells us many Samaritans were saved because of the woman's testimony. They urged Jesus to stay for several days so they might learn more. They credited the woman saying they believed not just because of what she'd told them but because they'd heard for themselves and believed he was the Christ.

Four years later, Philip the Evangelist came to Samaria to preach, and masses of people were healed and saved. He reaped a harvest that grew from the seed planted by the Samaritan woman.

Opening Prayer

Pray that God will use you to help reach others to him.

Scripture Reading

Read John 4:27–42 and Acts 8:5–8. Pay attention to what Jesus tells his disciples and what the Samaritans say about Jesus.

Review Questions

Why didn't the disciples say anything when they saw Jesus talking to the Samaritan woman?

Why did the woman leave behind her waterpot?

Who did she go to?

How did they respond?

Why didn't Jesus need food?

What did he mean about the seeds and the harvest?

Did the disciples understand what he was talking about?

Why did the Samaritans believe in Jesus?

Why was it such a big deal for Samaritans to believe that Jesus was the Messiah?

Scripture Memory Passage

Write out John 7:37–38 on an index card.

Closing Prayer

Ask God for opportunities for you to share the gospel with those around you.

DAY THREE: DIG DEEPER

The conversation between Jesus and the Samaritan woman is unusual on so many different levels, and yet, nothing about their conversation was random. God didn't see a debauched woman from an enemy territory. He saw a soul in need of saving.

Jesus understood how far this woman had strayed and knew she'd seen for herself how unsatisfying things of this world could be. He saw a woman with a receptive heart, searching for something this world couldn't provide. He knew she could more fully appreciate saving grace because of where she was coming from. He also knew the power her salvation would have on others. Once the Samaritans witnessed this woman's transformation, her new life would open the floodgates of opportunity for others. Jesus handpicked this woman to help initiate a spiritual awakening.

How might other women have acted in the situation? Would more respectable Samaritan women have avoided eye contact and limited any conversation with a Jewish man? They certainly wouldn't have countered his request with questions and engaged in a theological exchange. Proper women would know that behavior wasn't acceptable.

Jesus didn't mind the Samaritan woman's questions. In fact, he encouraged an honest discussion. He didn't expect her to have all the answers. He appreciated her open heart, wanting to know the truth. He not only answered her questions but revealed himself in a way he didn't often do.

Throughout the gospels, we see how Jesus penetrated cultural constraints and held deep and divine discussions with women. He recognized in women like the Samaritan woman a basic understanding of who he was and an eagerness to get to know him better. He encouraged women to think, to ask questions, to learn, and to grow in their spiritual walk.

Opening Prayer

Pray about any questions or concerns you have about God. Don't be afraid to ask honest questions. Be receptive to the answers.

Scripture Reading

Read John 4:7–26 in several Bible translations, paying special attention to the woman's questions and Jesus's answers.

Review Questions

Who initiated the conversation between Jesus and the Samaritan woman?

How did the woman initially act toward Jesus?

When did her attitude change?

Once she realized he was no ordinary man, what did she want to know?

Why did it matter to her where to worship?

How did the woman know about the Messiah?

How did she respond when Jesus told her who he was?

Scripture Memory Passage

Read aloud John 7:37–38 multiple times. How do these verses tie in with the Samaritan woman?

Closing Prayer

Pray for God to answer any questions or concerns you have about your faith.

DAY FOUR: MAKE IT PERSONAL

This is not a story of a woman seeking God, but rather him seeking her. Sometimes we are in such a place we don't feel comfortable reaching out to him. Your spiritual understanding may be so limited you don't know where to start or what to do. Or maybe you've sinned to the point you're embarrassed to address him due to your feelings of shame.

The good news is God knows our hearts. And though the world may have long ago dismissed you as too far gone, he doesn't see you that way. He sees past all your sins and sees you as someone in need of a savior.

Jesus purposely walked through Samaria and stopped at that specific well at that specific time because he knew she would be there. He knew she had reached the bottom and was looking upward. He saw her heart and perceived it was receptive. Jesus recognized her redemption would shine ever more brightly because she'd been so depraved in the past,. He saw in this woman the potential to reach many souls.

God sees you, and he longs to be there for you. He is able to redeem you from the life you've been living and lift you up from whatever depths you may have plunged to. He is ready and waiting to give you a living water so you will have eternal life and never thirst again. And then he wants to use you to reach out and draw others to him.

Opening Prayer

Ask God to forgive the sins of your past and to lead you to a new life with him.

Scripture Study

Research one of these passages using a Bible commentary, sermons, or original Hebrew. Make notes of what God is speaking to you through these passages.

- John 4:7–26
- John 7:27–38
- John 7:39–42

Listen to the All God's Women podcast episode or read the blog post on the Samaritan Woman.

Review Question

What do you have in common with the Samaritan woman?

How are you different from her?

What can you learn from her story?

How did the Samaritan woman know about God before her interaction with Jesus?

What does the Samaritan woman's story tell us about God's character?

How can you find encouragement in her story?

Are you as open with God as she was?

Are you as receptive to his teaching?

Are you sharing with others what you know about him?

Scripture Memory Passage

Read John 7:37–38 in multiple Bible versions. Place yourself in the place of Jesus's audience and write a response.

Example: "I am thirsty, let me drink from the eternal water ..."

Closing Prayer

Ask God to give you an excitement and love for him.

Day Five: Compare and Contrast

The Adulterous Woman

Religious leaders loved to place judgment on others. They elevated themselves and looked down on others. They didn't like that Jesus hung out with sinners and talked to women like the Samaritan woman.

The situation between Jesus and the authorities mounted. Many Jews sought to kill him. They were eager to find an opportunity to trick him so they might pronounce him guilty and get rid of him.

How did Jesus respond to the threats? By spending his nights in prayer and returning to the temple first thing in the morning. People gathered about him, so he sat down and taught them. While he was teaching, scribes and Pharisees brought to him a woman caught in the act of adultery. They led her front and center of the crowd and confronted Jesus.

[begin blocked quote]

Teacher, this woman has been caught in the act of adultery. Now in the Law, Moses commanded us to stone such women. So what do you say? (John 8:4–5)

[end blocked quote]

They thought they had him. Jesus was trapped. Whatever he said, they could turn against him. But Jesus said nothing. Instead, he stooped down and wrote on the ground, acting as if he hadn't heard them.

They persisted, asking him what should be done with her.

He stood up and addressed them. "Let him who is without sin among you be the first to throw a stone at her" (v. 7).

Then he bent back down and wrote on the ground again. While he wrote, they all left, from oldest to youngest. When he stood, the accusers were gone. Only the woman remained.

Jesus said, "Woman, where are they? Has no one condemned you?" (v. 10).

She said, "'No one, Lord.' And Jesus said, 'Neither do I condemn you; go, and from now on sin no more'" (v. 11).

As she went on her way, Jesus returned his attention to those he'd been teaching before the commotion and said, "I am the light of the world. Whoever follows me will not walk in darkness, but will have the light of life." (v. 12)

In biblical accounts of the Samaritan woman and the adulterous woman, we see two women openly living in sin, deserving of death, but redeemed by the mercy and love of Jesus.

Opening Prayer

Ask God to cleanse your heart and forgive you for past transgressions.

Scripture Reading

Read John 8:1–12. Make note of any similarities between this woman and the Samaritan woman as well as the response to those who witnessed Jesus's redemption of them.

Listen to the All God's Women podcast episode or read the blog post on the adulterous woman.

Review Questions

How are the Samaritan woman and the adulterous woman similar?

What are the differences between their stories?

What do the two women's interactions with Jesus have in common?

How were the two women's response to Jesus similar?

What was the difference between the reactions of other people to the women?

How did Jesus treat each of the women?

Did Jesus condemn them?

How did Jesus show mercy to the women?

What do these two women teach us about prayer?

What do they teach us about the character of God?

Scripture Memory Passage

Attach your Scripture memory index card to a water pitcher in your refrigerator. Every time you open your refrigerator, read it aloud.

Closing Prayer

Ask God to open your eyes to see people the way God sees them, seeing their hearts rather than their sins.

—Chapter Seven—
Bleeding Woman

Jairus, a ruler of the synagogue, fell at Jesus's feet and begged for healing for his twelve-year-old daughter who was at the point of death. He said he knew, if Jesus would just lay his hands on her, she would be healed and live. So, Jesus went with him, followed by a multitude of people. In that crowd was a woman who'd been bleeding for twelve years.

Wherever he went, Jesus was bombarded by the sick and afflicted, begging for his healing mercy. But this woman never did that. Instead, she found the most inconspicuous manner possible to be healed by Jesus. Not wanting to bother Jesus. nor call attention to herself, she didn't call on him to help her. Instead, she sought him out, then quietly reached out to touch the tassel on the hem of his cloak.

I'm sure she assumed, since she only touched his clothes and not his body, he'd never notice. But that kind of faith does not go unnoticed. In fact, her faith made such an impact that Matthew, Mark, and Luke each recorded the story of the bleeding woman and her healing.

DAY ONE: HER STORY

For twelve years, this woman had dealt with unexplained bleeding. She'd spent all her money on doctors and cures, but rather than healing her, they'd taken her money and left her in worse physical condition.

She had heard about Jesus and reasoned if she could just get close enough to Jesus to touch his clothes, she could be healed. So, when she heard he was passing through her area, that's what she did.

She made her way through the masses, and when she got near, she reached out and touched the tassel on his cloak. Just as she had thought would happen, immediately, her issue of blood dried up, and she sensed that she'd been healed. Jesus sensed it too because he felt the power leave him.

As the crowd pressed into him, Jesus stopped and turned around. "Who touched my garments?" (Mark 5:30).

Everyone stopped, wondering what he was talking about. His disciples pointed out the multitude surrounding him. Anyone could have touched him.

But he knew the difference. He looked around to see who would identify themself.

With fear and trembling, the bleeding woman stepped forward and fell at his feet, revealing the full story of what had happened. And with love and compassion, Jesus said to her, "Daughter, your faith has made you well; go in peace, and be healed of your disease" (v. 34).

While he was still speaking to her, a messenger came to Jairus to let him know his daughter had died. Undeterred, Jesus continued on his way to take care of another soul in need.

Opening Prayer

Ask God to give you the courage to step out in faith.

Scripture Reading

Read Mark 5:21–36. Make note of the circumstances of the bleeding woman's encounter with Jesus and his reaction to her.

Review Questions

What was Jesus doing when the bleeding woman went to him?

How long had the woman been bleeding?

What did the woman think to herself?

What did the woman do to receive healing?

What was Jesus's response to the woman?

What did the woman do when Jesus confronted her?

What did Jesus tell the woman?

Scripture Memory Passage

> Let us then with confidence draw near to the throne of grace, that we may receive mercy and find grace to help in time of need. (Hebrews 4:16)

Read aloud Hebrews 4:16. How does it relate to the story of the bleeding woman?

Closing Prayer

Pray for a specific need you have you may have been afraid to pray for because you're afraid to bring it to God.

DAY TWO: HER STORY IN CONTEXT

The religion and culture of Jesus's time consisted of hundreds of laws, many of which dealt with being clean and unclean. Blood was taboo. Women during their menstrual cycle were forced into seclusion as contact with a man would deem the man unclean. After their cycle or after childbirth, women underwent a special cleansing process before they were allowed to mingle again with society.

Because this woman had bled for twelve years, she'd not been able to go through the cleansing. Thus, she was deemed unclean and as a result, a social outcast.

To make matters worse, this woman had spent everything she had on doctors, but instead of helping, they'd made her situation worse. Not only was she an outcast, but also destitute and desperate.

A woman in her condition should not have been in a crowd of people. She was to avoid contact with others so she wouldn't contaminate them with her uncleanliness. She surely shouldn't touch a rabbi, and yet, she ignored the rules and came to Jesus anyway.

Better still, Jesus ignored the rules. He was more concerned with her faith than the legalistic abiding of the law. He saw her heart and healed her.

Opening Prayer

Ask God to help you see with your heart rather than your mind.

Scripture Reading

Read Leviticus 15:19–30. How do these verses relate to the bleeding woman's situation?

Review Questions

Why was the woman considered unclean?

What were unclean women supposed to do?

What happened if a man was exposed to an unclean woman?

What could have happened if the crowd had realized who the woman was?

How might other religious leaders have responded if an unclean woman touched them?

Why was Jesus not concerned?

What impact would her healing have on the woman's life?

Scripture Memory Passage

Write out Hebrews 4:16 on an index card and place it on your bathroom mirror.

Closing Prayer

Thank God for being a God of mercy and compassion.

DAY THREE: DIG DEEPER

Like the widow of Nain, the bleeding woman was a bonus healing. Each happened when Jesus was on his way to heal someone else. In this case, Jairus, a synagogue leader, approached Jesus to lay his hands on Jairus's daughter who was on the brink of death.

Just as Jesus knew the widow of Nain would be burying her son exactly when he and his followers were entering town, he also knew that this woman would be approaching him on his route to Jairus's house.

This was more than a mere healing. In allowing the bleeding woman to touch him and be healed, Jesus revealed his preference for compassion over legalism. What must the disciples have thought when they realized an unclean woman had been in their midst? Perhaps she'd touched them as she made her way to Jesus. Were they then unclean? But Jesus wasn't bothered. He could have chided the woman for disobeying the laws and coming to him. Instead, he praised her faith.

Opening Prayer

Ask God to open your eyes to what he would have you see and do.

Scripture Study

Reread Mark 5:25–34 then read Matthew 9:20–22 and Luke 8:43–46. Pay attention to what each writer reported in his account.

Make a chart to note details captured by each of the gospel writers. In one column note each detail captured by Matthew. In another note details captured by Mark. In the last column note details captured by Luke. Circle any details they all included.

Review Questions

Which details were recorded by each of the gospel writers?

How did the disciples know what the woman was thinking?

What was their response when Jesus asked who touched him?

How did they learn who touched him?

What must have gone through their minds when they learned an unclean woman was in their midst?

How did the crowd respond?

How did the woman respond?

Scripture Memory Passage

Every time you look at your index card recite Hebrews 4:16 aloud.

Closing Prayer

Pray for those around you who are silently hurting.

DAY FOUR: MAKE IT PERSONAL

Do you ever feel like an outcast, rejected by others, taken advantage of by those who were supposed to be helping you? If so, what a blessing it is to see how Jesus loved this woman.

Jesus didn't see her uncleanliness—only her purity of heart. He didn't condemn. He confirmed. He didn't blame. He encouraged. Jesus will do the same for you.

Perhaps you're waiting for Jesus to seek you. You're sitting in your comfort zone praying he will come and heal you. But what if he wants you to seek him? What if he wants you to reach out and touch him? Are you willing to do that?

We find waiting easy, reasoning if Jesus truly cared, he'd come to us. But what if he is waiting for us to take the first step?

Had the bleeding woman waited, she would have missed her healing. Jesus would have gone on his way to Jairus's house and the bleeding woman would have remained afflicted.

Stepping out in faith is scary, but our God is a loving God. He only wants what is best for you. Imagine going to him and hearing him say your faith has made you well, you've been healed from what afflicted you. Wouldn't that be worth the risk of taking your burden to him?

Opening Prayer

Ask God what he wants you to do in order to step out in faith.

Scripture Study

Use your study Bible, commentary, or online resources to find sermons or commentary on the bleeding woman. Read several viewpoints, noting what each commentator focused on and deemed important.

Listen to the All God's Women podcast or read the blog post on the bleeding woman.

Review Questions

What do you have in common with the bleeding woman?

How are you different from the bleeding woman?

What can you learn from bleeding woman's story?

What kind of interaction did the bleeding woman have with Jesus?

What did the bleeding woman know about God's power?

How can you find encouragement in the bleeding woman's story?

How do your interactions with God compare with the bleeding woman's?

Do you have the amount of faith the bleeding woman had?

Are you willing to proclaim your faith publicly despite any risks?

Has God ever healed you from an infirmity?

Scripture Memory Passage

Say aloud Hebrews 4:16 substituting "I" and "my" for "we" and "our."

Closing Prayer

Thank God specifically for answered prayers in your life.

DAY FIVE: COMPARE AND CONTRAST

Like the bleeding woman, the Shunammite woman needed a miracle and was willing to do whatever it took to receive that miracle.

The Shunammite woman's young son played in the fields with his father, but while he was there, he developed a terrific headache. The father instructed a servant to carry his son to his mother. She held him in her arms until noon that day. Then he died.

The woman carried him upstairs to Elisha's room and laid him on the bed. She closed the door behind her and asked her husband for a servant and a donkey so she might go to Elisha.

Her husband wanted to know why she needed Elisha since it wasn't the New Moon or the Sabbath. All she told him was, "All is well" (2 Kings 4:23).

She saddled her donkey and told the servant to go as fast as he could and not slow down unless she told him. Then they made the trek over twenty-five miles to Mount Carmel where she found Elisha.

Elisha saw her from a distance and sent Gehazi to greet her and to find out if all was well with her, her husband, and her son. She brushed him aside with, "All is well" and continued toward Elisha (v. 26).

When she reached Elisha, she fell to the ground and grabbed his feet, letting him know that something was wrong with her son. Elisha was set to send his servant to help her, but the woman told him she wouldn't leave until he came himself.

Her persistence paid off. Elisha went to her home and brought her son back from the dead. Like the bleeding woman, the Shunammite woman's faith resulted in a healing.

Opening Prayer

Continue to pray persistently for your needs.

Scripture Reading

Read the Shunammite woman's story in 2 Kings 4:8–37. Make note of similarities and differences in the story of the bleeding woman and the Shunammite woman.

Listen to the All God's Women podcast episode or read the blog post on the Shunammite woman.

Review Questions

How are the two women similar?

What are the differences between their stories?

Though the bleeding woman met directly with Jesus and the Shunammite turned to God's prophet, how were their interactions similar?

How did each of the women illustrate persistence and determination?

How were their outcomes similar?

What do these two women teach us about prayer?

What do they teach us about faith?

What do they teach us about the character of God?

Scripture Memory Passage

Share Hebrews 4:16 with others, whether in conversation, in a written message, or on social media.

Closing Prayer

Continue praying without ceasing, never giving up.

—Chapter Eight—
The Canaanite Woman

Both Matthew and Mark recorded the story of the Canaanite woman, and both authors precede her story by sharing Jesus's dispute with the Pharisees and scribes.

Religious leaders sought salvation through obedience to laws. They prided themselves on following to perfection each of the hundreds of petty laws. They were offended when others failed to follow those laws, especially Jesus and his disciples.

In this instance, their problem was the disciples ate food with unwashed hands. They pointed out to Jesus the laws of not only washing hands, but also washing cups, pitchers, copper vessels, and couches (Mark 7:4).

Jesus responded by pointing out the religious leaders focused on man-made laws rather than God-ordained commandments. He went on to share with his followers they need not worry about defilement which comes from food but rather defilement that comes from the heart.

Jesus needed a break after his discourse with the leaders and followers. He and his disciples traveled to the Tyre and Sidon region. Since this was pagan territory not inhabited by Jews, one would think they could escape from notice and get some much-needed rest. However, almost as soon as they arrived in Tyre, a Canaanite woman approached them and begged for Jesus to heal her demon-possessed daughter.

Like so many of the Bible women we've studied, this Canaanite woman knew of the Israelite God and recognized Jesus was his son. She knew he could heal her daughter, if only he would. This was a desperate situation. Her child was suffering. She wouldn't give up until her daughter was healed.

DAY ONE: HER STORY

Jesus needed to get away from the Pharisees and their harassment, so he took his disciples to the Canaanite region of Tyre and Sidon. Mark tells us they stayed in a house in Tyre and wanted no one to know they were there, but word leaked out.

A Canaanite mother heard Jesus was in town and learned where he was staying. She immediately went to the house, fell at his feet, and begged him to heal her severely demon-possessed daughter. We would expect Jesus at least to acknowledge her petition, but Matthew tells us Jesus ignored her, saying nothing.

The woman continued pleading until his disciples suggested he send her away because she was annoying them all. Instead, he finally addressed her pleas, saying, "I was sent only to the lost sheep of the house of Israel" (Matthew 15:24).

She wasn't deterred. Matthew 15:25 says she knelt before him, begging him to help her.

He responded, "It is not right to take the children's bread and throw it to the dogs" (v. 26).

His words sound harsh to us, but we know she didn't take it that way. She saw his words as a challenge of her faith, and she accepted the challenge. "Yes, Lord, yet even the dogs eat the crumbs that fall from their masters' table" (v. 27).

This Canaanite woman displayed a mighty faith and deep understanding of Christ's power and mission. Jesus couldn't help but commend her and heal her daughter. "O woman, great is your faith! Be it done for you as you desire" (v. 28).

Her daughter was healed from that moment.

What a contrast between the faith and understanding of Jewish religious leaders and the faith and understanding of this Canaanite mother.

Opening Prayer

Ask God to reveal to you his heart so you might see the situation as he sees it.

Scripture Reading

Read Matthew 15:21–28 and Mark 7:24–30. Note any differences between the accounts as well as the details that both writers included.

Review Questions

Why did Jesus go to Tyre and Sidon?

Where did the Canaanite woman find Jesus?

What was her petition?

What did the disciples think of her?

What was Jesus's response?

How did the woman respond when Jesus put her off?

What did Jesus say about her faith?

What happened to her daughter?

Scripture Memory Passage

I love the LORD, because he has heard my voice and my pleas for mercy. Because he inclined his ear to me, therefore I will call on him as long as I live. (Ps. 116:1-2)

Read aloud Psalm 116:1–2. How does it relate to the Canaanite woman?

Closing Prayer

Thank God for always hearing your prayers, though you may not always hear him.

DAY TWO: STORY IN CONTEXT

Matthew calls her a Canaanite. Mark refers to her as a "Gentile, of Syrophoenician descent" (Mark 7:26). According to the International Standard Bible Encyclopedia, this likely means she was a Canaanite from the Syro-Phoenicia area, and Greek was her language. Since Jesus's primary mission was to the Jews—she was not part of his ministry focus.

Israelites and Canaanites were sworn enemies. Their hostilities went back many centuries to the days of Moses. God told the Israelites that when they crossed over the Jordan River into Canaan, they were to drive out all inhabitants. He went on to say, "But if you do not drive out the inhabitants of the land from before you, then those of them whom you let remain shall be as barbs in your eyes and thorns in your sides, and they shall trouble you in the land where you dwell" (Numbers 33:55).

In Deuteronomy 7:2, God told them not to make covenants with Canaanites nor to show mercy on them. Why did he do this?

He explains in Deuteronomy 7:3–4.

> You shall not intermarry with them, giving your daughters to their sons or taking their daughters for your sons, for they would turn away your sons from following me, to serve other gods. Then the anger of the LORD would be kindled against you, and he would destroy you quickly.

Jesus's primary mission was to Jews, but that didn't mean he was heartless toward Gentiles. He came first to Jews but was slowly preparing them to accept he came to save both Jews and Gentiles.

We're all familiar with John 3:16. "For God so loved the world, that he gave his only begotten Son, that whosoever believeth in him should not perish, but have everlasting life" (KJV).

God was always open to those who truly believed in him. Think back to Rahab, Ruth, and others who came from pagan backgrounds but recognized the true God as their Savior.

When the Canaanite woman pleaded for Jesus to heal her daughter, she called him her Lord, the Son of David. In doing so, she acknowledged she knew who he was and believed in him as her Savior.

The Canaanite mother knew Jesus had the power to save her daughter, and she wasn't going to leave him alone until he'd done so. Imagine having that kind of faith and persistence.

Opening Prayer

When you pray, acknowledge God as your Lord and Savior.

Scripture Reading

Read Numbers 33:50–56, Deuteronomy 7:1–5, and Matthew 15:1–20. What do Old Testament laws have to do with Jesus and the Pharisees? What does any of this have to do with the Canaanite mother and her daughter?

Review Questions

Why did God order the Israelites to drive out the Canaanites from their land?

What else did he tell them to destroy?

Why did he tell them not to intermarry with the Canaanites?

What did he say would happen if they didn't listen to him?

What did Jesus point out that was wrong with the Pharisees and religious leaders?

What was wrong with their tradition?

What does all of this have to do with the Canaanite woman and her interaction with Jesus?

Scripture Memory Passage

Write out Psalm 116:1–2 in your journal or on an index card.

Closing Prayer

Read aloud Psalm 116 as your prayer.

DAY THREE: DIG DEEPER

At first glance, this interaction of Jesus with the Canaanite woman makes no sense. He spent his days talking about love, and yet he hardly seems loving toward this woman.

We need to read and reread this passage until God reveals to us what was really going on here.

First, why did Jesus ignore her at first, not responding to her pleas? Scripture is silent, but perhaps he was using that time to pray for wisdom and for the woman. Everything Jesus did was a teaching point for his disciples. They were watching his interaction with this Gentile woman and wondering how he'd react.

Was Jesus planning his words or perhaps testing the woman's faith, seeing if she would prevail through his silence. Most likely, it was for each of these reasons that Jesus took his time responding.

Jesus made clear to her he was sent for the Israelites, but she already knew that and didn't care. Her daughter was suffering, and the Jews' Messiah was the only one who could help her. So what if she wasn't an Israelite? She knew his heart, understood his character enough to realize he loved her and her daughter even though they were Gentiles.

To compare this woman and her daughter to dogs seems cruel to us, but she didn't take it that way. She knew he wasn't calling them wild animals but was instead referencing a beloved family pet. She grasped he was saying the Jews were his priority, but she knew he had plenty of healing power to spare. Like the bleeding woman, she was willing to take the fringes rather than expecting priority, because she knew it was enough.

She was right. Jesus saw the abundance of her faith. How could he not reward such trust by answering her prayer?

Opening Prayer

Ask God to reveal himself to you.

Scripture Reading

Reread Matthew 15:21–28 and Mark 7:24–30 using a different translation. As you read, focus on the dialogue between the woman and Jesus.

Review Questions

Why does the woman come to the house where Jesus is staying?

Why does she call out to him?

Why did Jesus not respond at first?

Why would Jesus treat her so coldly?

How does she interpret Jesus's comments to her?

Is she offended by Jesus?

Is Jesus offended by her persistence?

How does Jesus reward her persistence?

Scripture Memory Passage

Use your phone to record yourself reading Psalm 116:1–2 or say it aloud to a friend or family member.

Closing Prayer

Continue to pray even when it seems God isn't listening to you.

DAY FOUR: MAKE IT PERSONAL

This is one of those stories that used to make me feel uncomfortable. I didn't understand how Jesus could be a God of love, and yet treat this woman in a way I viewed as contemptible. I was reading this passage wrong. I wasn't taking into account the context of the story, the history of the Israelites and Canaanites, and Jesus's mission on earth. I also failed to notice the reaction of the woman.

Rather than viewing this as a discouraging story, if we read this passage in context, we can appreciate it as a story of hope and faith. This woman wasn't discouraged by her debate with Jesus, but instead, saw his words as a challenge. She rose to the occasion, victorious in her pursuit when Jesus provided healing for her daughter.

How often do we miss answered prayers because we fail to ask or because we give up too soon? The Bible contains reminders to keep presenting our prayers to God, even when it seems he's not listening. We must keep praying despite resistance. The harder it gets to pray, the more we need to push in and pray with even more fervor.

God loves us so very much and wants what's best for our lives. May we never forget that and grow weary in our prayers. Let us persevere until we receive a response from him.

Opening Prayer

Ask God to help you persevere in your pursuit of his best for your life.

Scripture Study

Read at least one commentary or sermon about the Canaanite woman. Read Matthew 15:21–28 and Mark 7:24–30 one last time to find any details you missed.

Listen to the All God's Women podcast episode or read the blog post on the Canaanite woman.

Review Questions

Why did both Matthew and Mark share this story?

What does this story reveal to us about God's character?

What does this story reveal to us about prayer?

What can we learn from this woman's interaction with Jesus?

Are you willing to go to God to meet your needs?

Do you trust that God will answer your prayers when it seems he's ignoring you?

Have you accepted Jesus as your Lord and Savior?

Is anything keeping you from reaching out to the Lord?

Scripture Memory Passage

Recite Psalm 116:1–2 aloud to the same friend or family member or pick someone new to share these verses. If you recorded it on your phone, listen to it throughout the day.

Closing Prayer

If you've not already done so, pray to accept Jesus as your Lord and Savior.

Day Five: Compare and Contrast

Rahab

Like the woman in this week's lesson, Rahab was a Canaanite. She came from the Amorite nation which was a pagan people. In fact, her name comes from an Egyptian god. However, like the woman from Syro-Phoenecia, Rahab heard about Jehovah and chose to seek him out however she could.

When the Hebrew spies entered Jericho, Rahab welcomed them into her house. When the king sent officers in search of those spies, Rahab hid the Hebrews on her roof. Once she sent the officers away, she approached the spies, sharing what she knew about their God and asking for their protection for herself and her family.

Like the Canaanite mother, Rahab acknowledged who God was and what he could do. She sought not only physical protection but eternal salvation for herself and her family. Rahab knew, though she wasn't part of God's chosen people, she could still choose to follow and worship him. So that's what she did, and God rewarded her faith by saving Rahab and her family when the Hebrew army overtook their city.

As if that weren't enough, he allowed Rahab to marry Salmon, a godly Hebrew man, and included Rahab in the lineage of Jesus. Perhaps the Canaanite woman knew about Rahab and drew encouragement from her story.

Opening Prayer

Thank the Lord for his forgiveness of your past sins and for the opportunity to start anew no matter how many times you fall short.

Scripture Reading

Read Joshua 2:1–21 and 6:22–25. Make note of any similarities between the two women, their situations, their response to God, and their petitions.

Listen to the All God's Women podcast episode or read the blog post on Rahab.

Review Questions

How are the Canaanite woman and Rahab similar? How are they different?

What were they wanting from God?

How did these women know about God?

What do these two women teach us about prayer?

What do they teach us about the character of God?

What do they show us about God's mercy?

How can we find encouragement from their stories?

Scripture Memory Passage

Share Psalm 116:1–2 with someone, either through conversation, a card, or a social media meme.

Closing Prayer

Pray without ceasing, never losing faith in God's love and mercy.

—Chapter Nine—
Martha

Poor Martha! How many sermons have been preached about Martha's shortcomings? How many books have been written encouraging women to be more like Mary and less like Martha? Because they were sisters, we feel a need to compare them to each other, but Martha and Mary were distinct individuals each worthy of study on her own.

Martha was one of several well-to-do single women who served Jesus and his disciples. When Jesus and his disciples traveled, they needed somewhere to rest their heads at night. While visiting the village of Bethany outside Jerusalem, they found refuge and rest at Martha's home. As they spent time in Bethany, they got to know Martha, her sister Mary, and her brother Lazarus, and the three siblings grew to know Jesus in a personal way. A close friendship developed.

Martha was a strong woman with a servant's heart. Her name means "lady" or "mistress of the house." Martha was a busy woman. A single woman, she carried the normal household responsibilities as well as hosting Jesus and his disciples whenever they came to Bethany. She shouldered a tremendous weight, and yet, in the midst of her work, Martha listened to Jesus and learned from him.

We first meet her, then her sister Mary, in the passage that's used to condemn Martha. We're told that Mary "was also seated at the Lord's feet and was listening to His word" (Luke 10:39 NASB). In other words, both Martha and Mary sat at Jesus's feet and listened to his teaching, but in this instance, only Mary sat while Martha worked.

Though Martha may have gotten caught up in earthly concerns in the first story, we see in Martha's conversation with Jesus at Lazarus's grave, the depth of her understanding of Jesus and his role on earth. She grasped his mission and what was to come in a way missed by most of his other followers. Martha obviously spent plenty of time listening and pondering the teachings of Jesus.

DAY ONE: HER STORY

The Bible provides us with three snapshots into the life and character of Martha. Luke 10 introduces us to Martha and her sister Mary. We're told that when Jesus and his disciples came to Bethany, Martha welcomed them into her house.

Right off, this tells us that Martha was a woman of distinction to have her own house. Was it because she was the eldest of the three siblings and thus inherited the family home? Was she a widow living in her husband's house? The Bible doesn't provide any background information, but from what Scripture does tell us, I believe we can assume Martha was an independent woman and a natural-born leader who took on responsibilities and burdens of those around her.

As we saw in Luke 10:39, Mary wasn't the only one who sat at Jesus's feet. Martha spent plenty of time there, but she was a busy woman with responsibilities. Jesus and his disciples needed to be fed, and who would feed them if not her? No wonder Martha was grumpy. She resented Mary doing what she wanted to be doing. If Mary would do her part, then the serving duties could go quickly and both sisters could spend time sitting and listening at Jesus's feet.

We see how comfortable Martha was with Jesus that she would take her family issue to him. Martha thought she knew Jesus well enough to predict how he would respond, expecting him to take her side and scold Mary for being lazy. Instead, Jesus chided Martha. He gently pointed out to her that though she was busy with worldly concerns, she should slow down and cherish the short time they had together.

How this must have stung Martha's pride. Here she was diligently serving him the best she knew how, and rather than praising her for her hard work, Jesus rebuked her for choosing work over worship. But did it make a difference? Did Martha take to heart his advice and devote more time to sitting and listening? I think she did, based on her next interaction with him.

Opening Prayer

Ask God to help you slow down to get to know him better.

Scripture Reading

Read Luke 10:38–42 in multiple Scripture versions. Make note of Martha's attitude in what she was doing.

Review Questions

Whose house did Jesus stay at when he was in Bethany?

Why was Martha distracted?

What did Martha say to Jesus?

What was Jesus's response to Martha?

What does this dialogue reveal about Martha's character?

What does this show us about Martha and Jesus's relationship?

What does it show us about the character of Jesus?

Scripture Memory Passage

> Set your minds on things that are above, not on things that are on earth. (Colossians 3:2)

Read and recite Colossians 3:2.

Closing Prayer

Ask God to give you wisdom to know what things are above and what are of the earth.

DAY TWO: HER STORY IN CONTEXT

We judge Martha by the scene when she complained to Jesus about Mary's laziness. However, look at her interaction with Jesus after her brother Lazarus died, and you see how much more there was to Martha and her relationship to Jesus.

In John 11, we're told that Lazarus got sick, and Martha and Mary sent word to Jesus to let him know. Verse 5 tells us Jesus loved Martha and her sister and Lazarus, but then verse 6 says he delayed travel for two days. By the time he arrived, Lazarus had already died and been in the tomb four days.

Martha and Mary were surrounded by friends comforting them in their time of sorrow, but as soon as Martha heard Jesus was coming, she ran to meet him. What amazing faith she exhibits as she shares that if Jesus had come earlier, her brother would still be alive, but regardless, she knows whatever Jesus asks of God, God will give him.

When Jesus tells her Lazarus will rise again, she assumes he means in the resurrection. This shows us she was paying attention when Jesus taught about the resurrection that was to come. But Jesus wasn't talking about the last days. He had something else in store for Lazarus, something much better.

Jesus explains to Martha in verses 25–26. "I am the resurrection and the life. Whoever believes in me, though he die, yet shall he live, and everyone who lives and believes in me shall never die. Do you believe this?"

She affirms with "Yes, Lord; I believe you are the Christ, the Son of God, who is coming into the world" (v. 27).

What amazing faith Martha exhibited. Soon after, however, when Jesus got to the tomb and asked for the stone to be rolled away, ever practical Martha pointed out

Lazarus's body would stink after being dead for four days. Jesus reminded her of their conversation, how he had told her if she would believe, she would witness the glory of God.

They rolled away the stone, and Jesus prayed aloud so all could hear. When he finished, he cried out for Lazarus to come out of the grave. And Lazarus did.

Martha knew Jesus could work miracles and trusted him for her eternal future, but didn't fully understand the extent of what he could do here on earth until she witnessed him raising her brother from the dead.

John 12 gives us one last glimpse at Martha. Jesus came to Bethany before the Passover, and Martha was back cooking and serving. She was no longer complaining, however. Instead, she was using her gifts to provide for Jesus in the way she knew best.

Opening Prayer

Pray for God to give you insight and understanding into his character.

Scripture Reading

Read John 11:1–27, 38–44; 12:1–2.

Review Questions

What did Martha do when she heard Jesus was coming?

How did she react to his delay in coming?

What did she think he meant when he said her brother would rise again?

What does this reveal about her understanding of Jesus?

Who did she say Jesus was?

How did she respond when Jesus asked for the tomb's stone to be removed?

What did Jesus say to her?

How did Martha show her appreciation to Jesus?

Scripture Memory Passage

Write Colossians 3:2 on multiple sticky notes and place them around your house to remind yourself to focus on things above rather than earthly cares.

Closing Prayer

Ask God to help you not to forget the things you already know about him.

DAY THREE: DIG DEEPER

Martha wasn't always running around cooking and cleaning. She was listening and observing and getting to know the character and mission of Jesus. She understood him in a way others didn't.

Jesus could have hurried to Bethany the moment he heard Lazarus was sick, but he didn't. Once he learned of Lazarus's death, he could have rushed to raise him from the dead, but he didn't. Instead, he took his time. John tells us Jesus delayed coming to their rescue because he loved Martha and Mary and their brother Lazarus.

Once Jesus arrived in Bethany, he could have gone directly to the tomb and resurrected Lazarus immediately. Instead, he took the time to engage in a deep theological discussion with Martha.

In a society where women were considered second-class citizens, unable to comprehend complex issues, Jesus saw women as worthy of spiritual conversations. He saw understanding and wisdom in Martha, so he used this opportunity to delve deep with her. What an honor and blessing he bestowed on her.

Opening Prayer

Ask God to help you dig deep in your understanding of who he is.

Scripture Reading

Read John 11:1–27, 38, and 44 in multiple translations. Pay special attention to what Martha says about the character of Jesus and what Jesus reveals about himself.

Review Questions

Why did Jesus delay going to Lazarus when he first heard he was sick?

How did Jesus feel about Martha and her siblings?

Why did the disciples warn him about going to Judea?

What difference do we see in Martha's attitude in this scene compared to when we first met her?

Why did Jesus stop to have this conversation with Martha?

Who did Martha say Jesus was?

Why did Martha resist when Jesus asked the tomb's stone to be rolled away?

Was it good for Martha to be serving when Jesus came to Bethany before the Passover?

Scripture Memory Passage

Every time you see your sticky note memory verse read it aloud.

Closing Prayer

Continue asking God to help you keep your focus on him and not on earthly cares.

DAY FOUR: MAKE IT PERSONAL

How often do we compare ourselves to those around us and find ourselves wanting? Jesus's rebuke of saying Mary had made the better choice could have hurt Martha's feelings. Instead, she realized he wasn't comparing them. He was merely reminding her to make sure she was focused on the things above rather than the cares of the world.

Imagine how different Martha's story would have been had she reacted in defense and fostered feelings of hurt and anger toward Jesus rather than accepting his words for what they were. She grew from his counsel.

Martha went on to take the time to listen to Jesus and to comprehend all he was teaching. When her brother died, she pulled from his teachings to realize that while the situation looked bleak, it didn't mean Jesus had forsaken them. In fact, Martha stood strong while those around her mourned. She focused on the eternal blessing of life after death, but Jesus surprised her by bringing back Lazarus from the dead and giving them more time together on earth.

The more we understand the character of God, the more equipped we are to handle life's setbacks. We understand they are only temporary and God has something greater for us in the future.

Opening Prayer

Thank God for answered prayers in your life when you thought the situation was hopeless yet he revealed himself to you in a mighty way.

Scripture Study

Read aloud John 11:4–5, 9–10, 26, and 40. As you read, imagine Jesus speaking directly to you.

Listen to the All God's Women podcast episode or read the blog post on Martha.

Review Questions

How are you like Martha?

Have you ever got so caught up in serving you forgot why you were serving?

Do you ever complain to God when life seems unfair?

Are you resentful of others who are worshipping while you're busy working?

Are you able to talk to God as you would a friend?

Do you listen when he talks to you?

Do you trust him when his actions don't make sense to you?

Do you run to spend time with him?

Do you sometimes forget his teachings amid worldly concerns?

Are you using your gifts to serve him as best you can?

Scripture Memory Passage

Recite Colossians 3:2 by memory.

Closing Prayer

Ask God to help you see anything you're doing that's keeping you from doing what he'd prefer you to do.

DAY FIVE: COMPARE AND CONTRAST

Dorcas

In the book of Acts, we find another independent woman like Martha who busied herself taking care of others. Dorcas, also known as Tabitha, was a disciple in Joppa. Acts 9:36 tells us she was full of good works and acts of charity.

Like Lazarus, Dorcas got sick and died. Since Peter was serving in Lydda about eight miles away, the other Joppa disciples sent two men to call for Peter to come immediately, which he did.

What did they hope to accomplish? Did they want him to show his respects? Did they ask him to perform the funeral? Were they expecting him to raise her from the dead? Probably not, as the disciples were not known to raise the dead.

Most likely Peter himself wasn't sure what he was to do. Nevertheless, he made haste and hurried to Joppa to the home of Dorcas.

When Peter arrived at her house, weeping women surrounded him, showing him the beautiful garments Dorcas had sewn for them. Peter ushered them all out of the upper room where Dorcas lay, then he knelt beside her and prayed. When he finished praying, he called out, "'Tabitha, arise.' And she opened her eyes, and when she saw Peter, she sat up" (Acts 9:40).

Peter helped her up, called to the saints and widows downstairs, and presented her alive.

As a result of her resurrection, many in Joppa believed in the Lord.

Opening Prayer

Ask God to use you to impact the lives of others.

Scripture Reading

Read Acts 9:36–43, making note of the similarities in the lives of Dorcas and Martha.

Listen to the All God's Women episode or read the blog post on Dorcas.

Review Questions

How are Dorcas and Martha alike?

How are they different?

How did they each serve those around them?

What impact did they have on others?

What kind of friend were they?

What similar challenges did they face?

How did Peter's response to Dorcas's death compare to Jesus's response to Lazarus's death?

How did God bless the two women?

What can we learn from these two women?

What do they teach us about the character of God?

Scripture Memory Passage

Share Colossians 3:2 with a friend, either through conversation, a handwritten note, or social media.

Closing Prayer

Ask God to give you a servant's heart.

—Chapter Ten—
Mary of Bethany

Mary of Bethany is often held up as a model of what we should do and who we should be like. How many of us have felt guilt over being more like Martha than Mary? We forget Mary was just a woman, like you and me, who had her strengths and weaknesses. Despite Jesus's praise for her, she had shortcomings. Her distinguishing feature, however, is her position at Jesus's feet.

The first time we meet her, Mary is sitting at Jesus's feet basking in his words of wisdom. She's in a position of learning. Next, she's falling at his feet, weeping over the death of her brother. We see her in a position of mourning. Our last picture is of her sitting at his feet anointing him with oil. In a position of utter humility, she's worshipping and serving him.

Mary didn't have all the answers, but she knew where to take her questions and concerns. No matter what was going on around her, Mary kept her eyes on Jesus. Humbling herself, she shut out the rest of the world. May we follow her example of spending time at the feet of Jesus.

DAY ONE: HER STORY

When Jesus came to Bethany, Martha busied herself taking care of his physical needs. Her sister Mary, however, sat glued to the floor at Jesus's feet, unaware of anything else going on around her. All she heard were the words Jesus shared.

We can imagine the scene. Martha brushes past Mary, mumbling complaints. Mary pays no attention. Martha storms out and bangs pots and pans in the kitchen, assuming this will get Mary's attention, but no such luck. Much time had likely passed by the time Martha reached her limit of patience and took her complaints to Jesus to settle.

We expect Mary to jump up and apologize for not doing her duty, but before she can respond, Jesus defends her actions, telling Martha Mary has chosen wisely to bask in the presence of the Lord, focusing all her attention on him.

A similar scene is repeated when Jesus returns to Bethany before his last Passover. Again, Martha serves, but this time Mary doesn't merely sit at Jesus's feet but pours a costly oil on his feet and wipes it with her hair. This time Judas complains about the expense of the oil, but again, Jesus defends Mary's actions.

Mary didn't care what others said about her. In fact, she doesn't appear to acknowledge them. She was so hyper-focused on her Lord, she blocked out anything else around her. Whatever else was going on, Mary knew all that mattered was what Jesus said and did. He didn't disappoint. Though others found fault, Jesus confirmed Mary was doing exactly what she needed to be doing.

Opening Prayer

Ask God to help you tune out distractions and focus on him.

Scripture Reading

Read Luke 10:38–42 and John 12:1–8. As you read, place yourself in Mary's position. Would you be able to block out the distractions and criticisms of others and focus completely on Jesus?

Review Questions

What do the two scenes with Mary and Jesus have in common?

How did others react to Mary's behavior?

Why was Martha upset with Mary?

Why was Judas upset?

How did Mary respond to their complaints?

How did Jesus respond to the complaints?

Scripture Memory Passage

Humble yourselves, therefore, under the mighty hand of God so that at the proper time he may exalt you casting all your anxieties on him, because he cares for you. (1 Peter 5:6–7)

Read aloud 1 Peter 5:6–7.

Closing Prayer

Go to a quiet place and pray for whatever is concerning you today.

DAY TWO: HER STORY IN CONTEXT

Sandwiched between the two scenes of Martha serving and Mary sitting at the feet of Jesus is the death of Mary and Martha's brother Lazarus. Jesus wasn't there when Lazarus got sick nor did he rush to them after he died. No, Jesus took his time coming, so Mary and Martha endured the task of burying their brother without the comfort of their friend Jesus.

Four days after the burial, friends surrounded Mary trying to comfort her. When Martha heard that Jesus had finally arrived, she hurried to him, but John 11:20 tells us that Mary remained in the house. Did she not realize he had come? Was she so busy with the others she didn't notice Martha running outside? Was she too busy mourning to notice what was going on around her?

Once Martha alerted Mary to Jesus's arrival, she did hurry to him, and when she reached him, she dropped down to her knees at his feet.

Mary repeats word for word what Martha had said to Jesus. "Lord, if you had been here, my brother would not have died" (John 11:32).

Martha continued with her statement of faith in Jesus, but Mary could only weep. Was she angry at Jesus? Did she feel betrayed by him? Did she share her sister's faith in the resurrection? We don't know. All we know is she cried uncontrollably, those who surrounded her cried, and Jesus, when he saw her tears, cried as well.

Opening Prayer

If you're harboring hurt or anger at God, take your concerns to him today.

Scripture Reading

Read John 11:17–38. As you read, make note of what this scene tells us about Mary, her character, her relationship with others, and her relationship with Jesus.

Review Questions

What did Mary do when Martha ran out to greet Jesus?

What did Mary do when Martha told her Jesus wanted to see her?

How did she respond to Jesus when she saw him?

How was Mary's response different from Martha's?

Why did Jesus weep?

Why was Jesus troubled?

Scripture Memory Passage

Write 1 Peter 5:6–7 on an index card.

Closing Prayer

Allow yourself the freedom to cry with Jesus over your sorrows.

Day Three: Dig Deeper

Every story in the Bible is included for a reason. Some are there to teach life lessons. Others show the impact of the actions of others. Many help us better understand ourselves. They all reveal to us aspects of the character of God.

Neither Luke nor John provides much information about Mary as an individual. However, they use her interaction with Jesus to reveal much about Jesus. We gain much insight into what he expects from us as believers in his treatment of Mary, in his defense of her actions, in his praise for her devotion.

Opening Prayer

Ask God to reveal himself to you in a personal way.

Scripture Study

Read Luke 11:39–42, John 11:6, 20, 28–37, 45, and John 12:3–7 in a different Bible translation, making notes of the interaction between Mary and Jesus and what their actions reveal about the character of Jesus.

Make a list of all the characteristics of Jesus that are revealed in his interactions with Mary and Martha and those around them.

Review Questions

How did Jesus feel about Mary and her siblings?

Why did Jesus defend Mary?

What did Jesus say about Mary?

Why didn't Mary immediately rush to Jesus like Martha did?

What did Martha tell Mary?

What influence did Mary have on those around her?

Why did Jesus cry with Mary?

What did Jesus say about Mary and her anointing oil?

Scripture Memory Passage

Place your 1 Peter 5:6–7 index card on the ground. Kneel and read the verses aloud.

Closing Prayer

Spend time just sitting and listening to what God is telling you.

DAY FOUR: MAKE IT PERSONAL

Mary wasn't a Bible scholar. She didn't have deep theological debates with Jesus. She wasn't setting the world afire with her go-getter attitude. We see no evidence Mary was anything but a simple woman who loved Jesus even though she didn't always understand him. And that was good enough.

We can easily read Scripture and feel overwhelmed by all we don't understand. We may want to give up on studying, feeling study is not worth our time. But in Mary's story, we see God doesn't expect us to have all the answers. He understands the limits of our comprehension. He knows we may not be able to present a deep theological explanation of our spiritual beliefs. But he assures us if we come to him with our undivided attention, soaking in all he wants us to absorb, he will take it from there. Though others may find fault in our devotion, he will take up our defense.

Opening Prayer

Pray over situations in your life you don't understand.

Scripture Study

Read aloud Luke 10:41–42, John 11:14–15, 33, 41–42, and 12:7–8. For each quote from Jesus, identify a name of God that relates. You may use the Names of God list in the appendices or do your own search to find other biblical names of God that are exhibited in these passages.

Listen to the All God's Women podcast or read the blog post on Mary of Bethany.

Review Questions

How are you like Mary?

How are you different from Mary?

When was the last time you spent time listening to God speak to you?

How much time do you spend at the feet of Jesus?

Do you go to God when you're angry with him for not answering your prayers the way you wanted them answered?

Do you take your tears to God?

How has God surprised you with an unexpected blessing?

Do you allow God to defend you or are you quick to defend yourself?

Do you allow God to weep with you?

Scripture Memory Passage

Turn 1 Peter 5:6–7 into a personal prayer.

Closing Prayer

Pray 1 Peter 5:6–7, thinking of specific examples in your life which apply.

DAY FIVE: COMPARE AND CONTRAST

Mary, Mother of Jesus

Mary of Bethany was a simple woman who sat at the feet of Jesus, taking in all he taught. She may not have understood all he said, but she trusted his every word.

Mary, the mother of Jesus, had that same trusting heart. As a young woman from a nondescript family, she didn't understand all the angel meant when an angel told her she would be the mother of the Christ child, but she trusted him. All she asked was how that could be since she was a virgin.

The angel explained to her the Holy Spirit would come upon her and overshadow her and that's how she would become a mother. He concluded with, "For nothing will be impossible with God" (Luke 1:37).

Mary responded to all this incredible information by simply replying, "Behold, I am the servant of the Lord; let it be to me according to your word" (v. 38).

When the shepherds arrived to worship her baby, and all marveled at what they shared, Mary "... treasured up all these things, pondering them in her heart" (Luke 2:19).

Both Marys share a humility and childlike quality that allowed them to take God at his word and to appreciate Jesus even when they didn't understand him. Both women loved him and spent time pondering his words. Both women held a special place in his heart.

May we learn examples of simple faith from the two Marys, striving to keep our eyes on him rather than worldly concerns, listening when he talks, pondering what he says, and keeping an obedient heart, obeying what he tells us to do.

Opening Prayer

Pray God will make his message known to you and you will accept his calling even if you don't understand it all.

Scripture Reading

Read Luke 1:26–38 and 2:1–20. Compare the faith of the two Marys.

Listen to the All God's Women episodes or read the blog posts about Mary, mother of Jesus.

Review Questions

How are the two Marys alike? How are they different?

How were their relationships to Jesus similar?

How were their relationships to Jesus different?

How did Jesus treat them?

How did Jesus watch out for them?

What can we learn from their interaction with Jesus?

What do they teach us about prayer?

Scripture Memory Passage

Share 1 Peter 5:6–7 with someone. Incorporate the verses into conversation, send a letter or message someone using this passage as encouragement or share it as a meme on social media.

Closing Prayer

Pray that you will have the faith to trust God even when you don't understand him.

Leader's Guide

While studying alone is great, sometimes it helps to join with others to study together. I meet many women who would like to have a group study but feel unqualified. I get it. I've been there. The thought of calling myself a Bible teacher terrified me.

I started by inviting a few women over for lunch and discussion, and before we ate, we'd talk about different women in the Bible. Our fellowship was relaxed and informal, with everyone enjoying themselves. Soon, though, I noticed they were calling our time together "Bible study," and I realized, in fact, that's what we were doing. Guess what! I realized leading a Bible study wasn't a big deal after all.

Group Bible study doesn't have to be scary. You don't have to have a seminary degree nor be fluent in Greek and Hebrew to be able to lead women in discussion about Scripture that you've all read.

If you've done Bible studies in the past, you might find the Women of Prayer format a little different. Rather than covering large amounts of material, we're zooming in on targeted passages about women in the Bible and their interactions with God. We start off with introducing each woman. Then we read her story. From there, we go deeper, putting her story in the bigger context, and then studying her circumstances in a way that brings the message home in a personal way. We close by taking the prayer concepts and study techniques covered and applying them to a different woman.

I've written this study to help each woman learn to study the Bible on her own. To get the most out of this material, each woman should have the freedom to pursue her studies in whichever direction God leads her. She's not confined to simply filling in blanks, but instead, going off on God-ordained rabbit trails as long and as winding as she wants to go.

You won't have women avoiding the meetings because they didn't finish their assignment, because even if a woman only reads the first day or two, she'll still be able to join in the conversation. And then, chances are, after listening to other women talk about their own studies, she'll get encouraged to go back and study more on her own.

So, while you may all be reading about Hagar, each woman will get something different out of her story. Some will focus on her as a slave. Some will get caught up in the drama between Hagar and Sarai. Others will be fascinated by Hagar's conversation with God. Each will be excited about what she read and learned, and their excitement will be contagious.

With a relaxed format and with women able to explore in different directions, you don't have to feel like a teacher at all. You're merely providing the setting and getting the conversation started. Then they'll take it from there. You can consider yourself a facilitator rather than a teacher. You can do this!

Getting Started

If you'd like to have your own Women of Prayer home Bible study, here are guidelines to get you started.

Create a Group

Who do you want to share this study? You can handpick women to join your group or put out a call on social media or through your church. You might consider a neighborhood group, in which case, you can send out invitations to all the women on your street or block. You can even do a virtual group with women around the world. Since this is your group, you get to decide what works best for you.

I encourage you to use this as an opportunity to expand your borders. Don't just invite a group of women who are already used to hanging out together. Invite at least one woman you don't know well. Try to include a range of women—young and old, married and single, introverts and extroverts. You'll find diversity makes for much more interesting conversations and new insights.

Set a Day and Time

Pick a meeting time that works for you as well as the women in your group. Select an evening time if you're a working woman and other women in your group work during the day. You may prefer to meet in the mornings or early afternoons if you're retired or have flexible hours. You have many options since so many women work from home now. Take a poll and find what time works best for your group of women.

Determine which day of the week works best as well. Work around any regular events affecting your women, and don't schedule a time conflicting with any major ministries at your church.

Decide how often you want to meet. Will you do weekly, every other week, once a month? While weekly is great, you may find more women will come if they only need to commit to every other week. The downside is then you'll need to remind them each week because women tend to lose track of which week you're meeting.

Determine a Location

Where will you meet? The most logical choice is your house, but if you're not comfortable meeting there, that's fine. There are plenty of other options. You can always meet at church or a public meeting room at the library. You might consider meeting in a coffee house or restaurant if you want to involve women outside your church. The first women's Bible study I attended as a young newlywed was held in a park. Many of the women had children, so the teen siblings kept an eye on the younger children while we had our discussion around a picnic table.

If meeting at a church or business, be sure to get permission ahead of time and choose a time convenient for the venue as well as attendees.

An additional option is to have virtual meetings, but while virtual can be a great lifesaver in some situations, meeting in person is always best if you can. Seeing each other on screens doesn't compare to sitting side by side.

Keep in Touch

Once you have your group, be sure to keep them updated, reminding them of the meetings, and following up with them to make sure they don't get distracted and forget. Remind them too of which woman you're studying that week.

Set Guidelines

Decide in advance if you want an open or a closed group. Do you want women to invite friends? Do you want to grow? Would you rather stick to an intimate group that doesn't change?

Either way works but knowing in advance helps so you're not caught off guard when extra women show up at your doorstep.

Prepare

While you're not going to be teaching per se, you still want to be familiar with the material prior to starting the study. You want to have gone through the study on your own so you know what to expect. Then, you'll want to refresh your memory the day before your group gathers.

Prayer

I know you know this, but I'm going to remind you anyway; You can't do a Bible study on prayer without spending time in prayer. Pray beforehand. Pray during your study time. Pray afterward. Pray for yourself and for the women in your group. Pray for wisdom and insight. Pray God will reveal himself to you. Pray each of you will grow in your spiritual walk.

WEEKLY GUIDELINES

I want you to be able to do your own thing, but sometimes you need a little nudge in the right direction to get you going. Consider these suggestions. Use them as a launching point, but feel free to deviate to best serve your individual group.

The women will have already read the Scripture at home but consider reading the focal passages aloud. When reading aloud, you'll often catch things you may not have noticed before. Be sure, though, to check with women beforehand. Not every woman is comfortable reading aloud in front of others.

The same goes for prayer. Don't embarrass someone by asking her to pray if you're not confident she will be fine with it.

I like to have the Scripture passages written on sheets of paper. As women arrive, ask them if they'd feel comfortable reading, and if so, I hand them the paper with the verses to look up in their Bible. For prayer, just ask ahead of time if they would be willing to either open or close in prayer. That way they have time to prepare what they might say.

Don't limit yourself to each week's guidelines. Create your own questions. Skip questions altogether. Use icebreakers if you want to get to know the women better. Jump right in if you want to spend more time in Bible discussion.

Each group will be different, so take whatever your women bring to the table and use it to further your Bible study. Be willing to adapt each week as needed for your women to get the most out of a study.

Don't worry if a woman brings up something you hadn't considered. Praise her insightfulness, then either respond by saying you had not previously thought of this point, but you will try to find the answer before the next meeting, or stop right there and try to find the answers before moving forward. I think you'll find your women will enjoy the challenge of searching for answers together.

Your primary objective as a group facilitator is getting women studying the Word. There's no right or wrong way to motivate every group, so do what works best for your group and feel free to deviate from the plan as God leads.

INTRO SESSION

Depending on your schedule or setup, you may want to begin with an intro session before launching into the Bible study. This is optional but may help the women get introduced and comfortable with each other before starting the Bible discussion. Since this won't take long, you have a perfect excuse to serve refreshments so women can fellowship and get better acquainted.

Welcome

If possible, have women sitting in a circle. This allows for the best conversation and discussion. Have each woman go around the circle and introduce herself by sharing which Bible woman they feel is most like them.

Opening Prayer

Pray for God to work through the Scripture study and group meetings to guide each woman and help her to grow in the Lord.

Study Time

Introduce the study. Explain that each week, they will study a different woman who interacted with God. From those interactions, they will gain understanding of themselves as well as get to know better the character of God.

Depending on your group, you may want to have on hand study Bibles, parallel Bibles, commentaries, or other Bible study reference books. You may also have them pull out their phones and show them how to find Bible study websites like Bible Hub, Bible Gateway, and Blue Letter Bible.

While they have their phones out, take them to www.allgodswomen.com and show them how they can search for podcast episodes and blog posts on each woman you'll be studying.

Next Meeting

Let the women know that at your next meeting, they will study Hagar. Guide them through the format and answer any questions they have.

Closing Prayer

Close each session in prayer, asking God to speak to each of you and reveal to you what he wants you to learn.

WEEK ONE — HAGAR

Open

Begin the session by going around the circle and having each woman share a time when God revealed himself to her. Keep the answers to a sentence or two, not allowing anyone to monopolize the time. Feel free to interject as needed to make sure each woman has time to share.

Prayer

Ask God to guide your time together and use it to reveal himself to you in a mighty way.

Read

Have three volunteers read Genesis 16:7–13. Assign one to be the narrator, one to read Hagar's words, and another to read God's words.

Discussion

Here are possible questions to ask to get discussion started. Don't feel a need to cover each question. Let God take the lead. Tailor your discussion to the needs of your individual group of women.

1. What did you learn about Hagar you didn't know before?
2. What did you learn about God? About yourself?
3. What resources did you use to study Hagar? Which did you find most helpful?
4. How does Psalm 139:1–2 tie in with Hagar's story?

Close

Recite Psalm 139:1–2 together. Encourage them to incorporate the passage in conversation with others.

Remind them next week they will study Miriam.

Prayer

End your meeting with prayer.

WEEK TWO — MIRIAM

Open

Have each woman share a time when God got her attention. Again, make sure each woman knows to limit her answer to a sentence or two.

Prayer

Ask God to speak to your hearts.

Read

Read Numbers 12 aloud. Have one volunteer read Numbers 12:1–5, another read vv. 6–8, another vv. 9–13, and another vv. 14–16.

Discussion

Using these possible questions, tailor your discussion to the needs of your individual group of women.

1. What did you learn about Miriam you didn't know before?
2. What did you learn about God? About yourself?
3. What names of God relate to God's interaction with Miriam?
4. How was God's treatment of Miriam and Eve similar?
5. Why must God be a God of judgment?
6. How does Ephesians 4:29 tie in with Miriam's story?

Close

Recite Ephesians 4:29 together before closing in prayer. See if anyone can recite the verse by memory.

Remind them next week they will study the daughters of Zelophehad.

Prayer

Always end meetings with prayer.

WEEK THREE — DAUGHTERS OF ZELOPHEHAD

Open

Ask each woman to go around the circle and share about an inheritance, either something they inherited or something they plan to pass on as an inheritance.

Prayer

Ask God for wisdom in discerning his will for your lives.

Read

Have one woman read aloud Numbers 27:2–4. Have another woman read Numbers 27:5–6, and another woman read Numbers 27:7–11.

Discussion

Consider these questions or others you think of to lead your discussion time.

1. What did you learn about the daughters of Zelophehad ?
2. What does their story show us about God's character?
3. Why was this story revolutionary at its time?
4. What does this show us about God's opinion of women?
5. What is your takeaway from this story?
6. How does John 15:7 tie in with the daughters of Zelophehad's story?

Close

Ask if anyone can recite John 15:7 by memory. Allow each woman to try.

Let the women know they will study Deborah next week.

Prayer

End your meeting by joining together in a circle and holding hands (or putting arms around each other) and praying together.

WEEK FOUR — DEBORAH

Open

Ask each woman to go around the circle and share a time when they had to be brave. Since this topic may lean toward lengthy responses, try to keep women on topic and keep the conversation moving.

Prayer

Ask God to give each woman wisdom and discernment and the courage to do what God asks them to do.

Read

Read Judges 5:2–11 aloud. You can have one woman read it all, or there are many ways to break it up. Perhaps have a different reader for each verse. For added fun, after each verse have the women stand up and say, "Praise the Lord!"

Discussion

1. What did you learn about Deborah you didn't know before?
2. Why did God choose her to lead his people?
3. Are you more like Deborah or Barak in obeying God?
4. What does Deborah's story show us about God's character?
5. What does Deborah's story show us about God's attitude toward women?
6. How does James 1:5 tie in with Deborah's story?

Close

Recite James 1:5 together by going around the circle with each woman saying a word. See how quickly you can say the verse together. Maybe several repetitions, going a little faster each time.

Let women know they will study Hannah next week.

Prayer

Close your meeting with prayer for God to give each woman courage to do what God calls her to do.

WEEK FIVE — HANNAH

Open

Ask women to go around the circle and share about a prayer they had prayed for many years.

Prayer

Pray for unspoken prayers for each of each woman.

Read

Read aloud 1 Samuel 2:1–10. For added drama, pull up an instrumental version of a hymn and play it softly in the background during your time of reading Scripture.

Discussion

1. Have you ever felt discouraged like Hannah?
2. Do you remember to praise God?
3. Do you ever praise God before he's answered your prayers?
4. How are you like Hannah?
5. How were the days Hannah lived in similar to today?
6. What does Hannah's story show us about God's character?
7. What is your takeaway from Hannah's story?
8. How does Psalm 18:6 tie in with Hannah's story?

Close

Ask if anyone has memorized Psalm 18:6. If they have, get them to recite it to the group. Read the verses aloud together if no one has memorized the Scripture.

Let the women know next week they will study the Samaritan woman.

Prayer

Close by praying a prayer of praise.

WEEK SIX — SAMARITAN WOMAN

Open

Go around your circle and share a question you would ask Jesus if you were to meet him in person like the Samaritan woman.

Prayer

Pray that God will answer any questions you have about him.

Read

Read aloud John 4:7–26 reading only lines of dialogue. Have one woman reading the words of the Samaritan woman and another woman reading the words of Jesus.

Discussion

1. What did you notice about the Samaritan woman you never noticed before?
2. What does their conversation tell us about what Jesus saw in the Samaritan woman?
3. What does the Samaritan woman's interaction with Jesus reveal about the character of Jesus?
4. As you read and studied, did you gain a better understanding of the Samaritans and Jews?
5. What can you learn from the Samaritan woman's story?
6. How does John 7:37–38 tie in with the story of the Samaritan woman?
7. What is your takeaway from this story?

Close

Read together John 7:37–38. Share what the passage means to you.

Prayer

Divide into prayer partners. Pray together with your partners.

WEEK SEVEN — BLEEDING WOMAN

Open

Go around the circle and have each woman share an answered prayer.

Prayer

Thank God for the answered prayers they shared.

Read

Read aloud Mark 5:27–34. Break it up with one woman serving as narrator, another as the bleeding woman, one as Jesus, and one as the disciples. Have your narrator reading the narrative and the others reading lines of dialogue.

Discussion

1. Have you ever felt unclean and unworthy of approaching Jesus?
2. Did you approach him anyway?
3. Do you ever feel lost in the crowd?
4. In your research, what did you learn that helped you better understand the miracle?
5. What does Jesus's response to the bleeding woman show us about his character?
6. What is your takeaway from the bleeding woman's story?
7. How does Hebrews 4:16 relate to the healing of the bleeding woman?

Close

Read aloud Hebrews 4:16, substituting "I" and "my" for "we" and "our."

Prayer

Pray for each of the women to have the courage to draw near to God.

WEEK EIGHT — CANAANITE WOMAN

Open

Go around the circle and have each woman either share about an unanswered prayer request she's been praying about for a long time or else one God answered after much persistence on her part.

Prayer

Pray for the long-term prayer requests. Thank God for the answered prayers.

Read

Read aloud Mark 7:24–30. Have one woman serve as narrator, one reading the words spoken by the Canaanite mother, and one reading words of Jesus.

Discussion

1. What was your first response to this story?
2. How did your view change as you studied the story more in-depth?
3. How did it help you to learn more about the culture and background?
4. Do you have the courage and persistence of the Canaanite woman?
5. What does this story show us about Jesus, his mission, and his character?
6. What is your takeaway from the Canaanite's experience?

Close

Read aloud Psalm 116:1–2. Have women share how the verse has ministered to them?

Prayer

Ask if any woman who's been afraid to pray aloud will take the risk and close in prayer.

WEEK NINE — MARTHA

Open

Go around the circle and have each woman share something that God is teaching her.

Prayer

Pray for God to continue to reveal himself to the women in the group.

Read

Read aloud John 11:21–27. Ask two women to read the lines of dialogue, one reading the lines by Martha and the other reading the words of Jesus.

Discussion

1. What did you learn about Martha you'd never noticed before?
2. What do her words reveal about her understanding of Jesus and his mission?
3. Which Martha scene do you most relate to?
4. Are you ever guilty of serving when you should be studying or worshipping?
5. Do you trust God when things don't go the way you think they should?
6. What is your takeaway from Martha's story?
7. How does Colossians 3:2 relate to Martha?

Close

Recite together Colossians 3:2.

Prayer

Pray God will help each woman to focus on things above rather than things on earth.

WEEK TEN — MARY OF BETHANY

Open

Go around the circle and ask each woman to share a personal encounter with God, a time when she felt particularly close to him.

Prayer

Gather together and hold hands for prayer time. Pray for God to draw each woman nearer to him.

Read

Read aloud Luke 10:39–42, John 11:32–35, and John 12:3–7.

Discussion

1. How much time do you spend at the feet of Jesus?

2. Are you willing to spend time with God when others don't understand what you're doing?

3. Do you have faith like Mary?

4. What have you learned about Mary you never thought of before?

5. What does Mary's interaction with Jesus reveal about God's character?

6. What name of God best describes your relationship with him?

7. What is your takeaway from Mary's story?

Close

Read aloud 1 Peter 5:6–7. Break into pairs and read the verse to each other.

Prayer

Gather in a huddle and pray silently for each other. After a time of silent prayer, invite women to pray aloud if they'd like.

CLOSING SESSION

Consider having an optional gathering to celebrate the completion of your study.

Depending on your meeting time, you might want to host a covered dish luncheon or dinner or serve finger foods or desserts.

If you want to play games, create a Women of the Bible trivia game.

Encourage women to launch their own Women of Prayer Bible study with a few friends.

About the Author

Through the years, Sharon Wilharm has worn many hats—filmmaker, blogger, writer, ministry leader, speaker, podcaster, and radio host. The common thread of all her hats is women and storytelling.

Sharon loves to tell stories to inspire and encourage women in their walk with the Lord. As a filmmaker, she made Christian movies with a female perspective. As a blogger, she's shared the stories of female filmmakers, actresses, authors, and speakers. As a ministry leader, she's worked with girls and women of all ages.

Once Sharon discovered Bible women and started telling their stories, she truly found her voice. She fell in love with the Bible and the stories within its pages. Now she can't stop talking about all the amazing women of the Bible and how much we have in common with them.

All God's Women, Sharon's podcast and syndicated radio show, takes listeners on a journey through the Bible, one woman at a time. *All God's Women* reaches listeners around the world and is broadcast on over a hundred radio stations including the Moody Radio Network. Learn more about Sharon and her ministry at www.sharonwilharm. com.

Appendices

NAMES OF GOD

The God Who Sees Me
The Lord Will Provide
Mighty Creator
Deliverer
The Everlasting God
The Lord Who Heals
Lamp
Alpha and Omega: The Beginning and End
Counselor
The Lord My Banner
The Lord My Rock
The Lord Is Peace
My Refuge
Lord and Judge of All the Earth
Our Shepherd
Everlasting Father
King
The Lord Is There
Our Advocate
The Author of Life
Bridegroom

HELPFUL RESOURCES

To assist in your study of women in the Bible, I compiled this list of resources I've found helpful. You'll find each one approaches the subject from a different angle. By reading from multiple sources, we gain a better understanding of the people and places, so when we pour into the Bible, we notice details we didn't notice before.

Devotional and Study Bibles

Holy Land Illustrated Bible. (Nashville: Holman, 2020). Contains articles about life during biblical times.

(in)courage Devotional Bible, (Nashville: Holman, 2018). Includes profiles of fifty women in the Bible.

The Study Bible for Women. (Nashville: Holman, 2015). Features articles and study notes related specifically to women and their roles in Scripture.

The Tony Evans Study Bible. (Nashville: Holman, 2019). Filled with helpful study notes to help you gain understanding of the Scriptures.

The Woman's Study Bible. (Nashville: Thomas Nelson, 1995). In addition to study notes throughout the Bible, this edition has short biographies of Bible women as well as articles related to woman during Bible times.

Women of the Bible Books

Bream, Shannon. *The Women of the Bible Speak.* (New York: Broadside Books, an imprint of Harper Collins, 2021). Life lessons from sixteen women in the Bible.

Deen, Edith. *All the Women of the Bible.* (New York: Harper One, an imprint of Harper Collins, 1998). This is my second favorite Bible women book. The author includes detailed bios of the main women as well as shorter listings for the obscure women.

Donadio, Angela. *Fearless: Ordinary Women of the Bible who Dared to do Extraordinary Things.* (Alachus, FL: Bridge-Logos Inc., 2019). A six-week Bible study about women who dared to do extraordinary things.

Freeman, Lindsay Hardin. *Bible Women: All Their Words and Why They Matter.* (Cincinnati: Forward Movement, 2014). Focuses on the words spoken by women in the Bible thorough study of all the different women mentioned in the Bible.

Higgs, Liz Curtis. *Bad Girls of the Bible.* (New York: Waterbrook Press, an imprint of the Penguin Group, 1999). A look at Bible women by relating them to modern women.

Lockyer, Herbert. *All the Women of the Bible.* (Grand Rapids: Zondervan Academic, 1988). If I could only have one book about women in the Bible, this would be my choice.

Mathers, Alice. *A Woman God Can Use.* (Grand Rapids: Our Daily Bread Publishing, 2018). Stories of Bible women that can help women today make wise choices.

McArthur, John. *Twelve Extraordinary Women.* (Nashville: Thomas Nelson, 2005). In-depth analysis of twelve Bible women.

McLelland, Kristi. *Jesus and Women.* (Nashville: Lifeway Press, 2020). A Bible study about Jesus and his interactions with women.

Murphy, Latan Roland. *Courageous Women of the Bible.* (Ada, MI: Bethany House, 2018.) Biblical studies of twelve women in the Bible.

Richards, Sue, and Larry Richards. *Every Woman in the Bible.* (Nashville: Thomas Nelson 1999). An encyclopedia-style study of the Bible women and the world they lived in.

Smith, Jill Eileen. *When Life Doesn't Match Your Dreams: Hope for Today from 12 Women of the Bible.* (Ada: MI: Revell, 2019). Stories of hope centered on twelve Bible women.

Spangler, Ann. *Wicked Women of the Bible*. (Grand Rapids: Zondervan, 2015). Stories of twenty women who were wicked good or wicked bad.

Spangler, Ann, and Jean E. Syswerda. *Women of the Bible*. (Grand Rapids: Zondervan 1999). A one-year devotional study of Bible women.

Swaggart, Jimmy. *Great Women of the Bible New Testament*. (Winona, MS.: World Evangelism Press, 2014). Interesting read about women in the New Testament.

Swaggart, Jimmy. *Great Women of the Bible Old Testament*. (Winona, MS.: World Evangelism Press, 2013). Interesting read about women in the Old Testament.

Tucker, Ruth A. *Dynamic Women of the Bible: What We Can Learn from Their Surprising Stories*. (Ada, MI: Baker Books, an imprint of The Baker Group, 2014). A comparison of twenty-four pairs of Bible women.

Additional Study Helps

Blaiklock, E. M. *Today's Handbook of Bible Characters*. (Ada, MI: Bethany House, 1987). Seven hundred and forty studies of men and women in the Bible.

Gower, Ralph. *The New Manners and Customs of Bible Times*. (Chicago: Moody, 2005). Pictures and illustrations along with text about life during Bible times.

Lockyer, Herbert. *All the Men of the Bible*. (Grand Rapids: Zondervan 1988). Companion to *All the Women of the Bible* when you need to learn more about the men in the stories.

Nelson's Complete Book of Bible Maps and Charts. (Nashville: Thomas Nelson, 2022). Charts and Tables for each book of the Bible.

Packer, J. I., Merrill C. Tenney, and William White Jr. *Nelson's Illustrated Encyclopedia of Bible Facts*. (Nashville: Nelson Reference & Electronic Pub, an imprint of

Thomas Nelson, 1995). A reference book about everyday life during Bible times.

Wight, Fred H. *Manners and Customs of Bible Lands*. (Chicago: Moody, 1994). Descriptions of housing, food, family life, religious life, and more during Bible times.

www.ingramcontent.com/pod-product-compliance
Lightning Source LLC
Chambersburg PA
CBHW060013100426
42740CB00010B/1474